Write *English* Right

An ESL Homonym Workbook

- contains both practice exercises and tests -

by

Lawrence Klepinger, M.A. Ed.

BARRON'S

All inquiries should be addressed to:
Barron's Educational Series, Inc.
250 Wireless Boulevard
Hauppauge, New York 11788

Library of Congress Catalog Card No: 92-40533

ISBN-13: 978-0-8120-1462-4
ISBN-10: 0-8120-1462-6

Library of Congress Cataloging-in-Publication Data

Klepinger, Lawrence.
Write English Right : an ESL homonym workbook / by Lawrence Klepinger.
p. cm.
Includes index.
ISBN 0-8120-1462-6
1. English language—Homonyms—Problems, exercises, etc. 2. English language—Textbooks for foreign speakers. I. Title.
PE1595.K58 1993
428.2'4—dc20 92-40533
CIP

PRINTED IN THE UNITED STATES OF AMERICA
12 11 10 9 8

TABLE OF CONTENTS

TO THE STUDENT

Write English Right will help you:

1. clear up many of the frequently asked questions about words, their proper spelling, and usage.
2. develop an easy method of vocabulary building that is essential to a good command of the English language. For example, when you learn the words **cite / sight / site**, only one pronunciation is needed but three meanings are learned. This is a convenient method for building your conversational ability.
3. learn word definitions which have purposely been kept simple and easy to understand. For your convenience, grammatical explanations have also been simplified.
4. memorize many of the example sentences that can be used in everyday conversation.
5. remember useful information contained in many of the example sentences. This way you add to your general knowledge while you learn a second language.
6. clear up questions that might come up during your studies, by referring to the **Note** section of the text for quick reference and thorough understanding.

Write English Right is so simple to use it is almost self-explanatory. It is organized in alphabetical order so all you have to do is look up a word that you are having trouble with just as you would in a dictionary.

The quickest way to look up a word is to check the alphabetical index in the back of the book to locate the word, then turn to the page number indicated in the index and start to work.

Each entry in *Write English Right* is organized into three parts. The first part presents the homonyms, gives a brief definition for each, and shows you how they can be used in sentences. The second part asks you to insert the correct word in a given sentence. The third part is for writing your own sentences. The asterisks and boxed area indicate words previously presented and can be used for quick reviews.

The book is divided into three sections, each followed by a Section Review to test your understanding of the words learned. Although the review covers terms presented up to that point, it is not necessary to study these terms in any certain order. In fact, the review can help you identify words that are still giving you trouble. Finally, at the end of the book is a Comprehensive Review designed to evaluate the progress you have made.

TO THE INSTRUCTOR

Write English Right provides an easy method to help your students:

1. use similar sounding words in their proper context in everyday conversation (hearing, speaking).
2. build their vocabulary comprehension (reading).
3. use the same or similar sounding words correctly in English composition and improve their spelling at the same time (writing).

The book's page by page systematic instruction and practice exercises allow your students to write their own sentences in the book itself. This eliminates the problem of loose papers and makes correcting easy.

It is organized so that skipping pages deemed unnecessary presents no problem to your students. Learning can take place using any part of the book. One page is not dependent on another.

ACKNOWLEDGMENTS

I would like to express my appreciation to the following people for helping to make this book possible.

Paul Abbott and Professor David Kluge for lending a hand every time I got stuck with my computer and threatened to throw it out the window.

Alice Parker for her tireless effort in reading the manuscript numerous times, pointing out problems and helping to iron out mistakes.

Professor Lawrence E. Kelly for giving me the impetus to "get the thing done."

Professor Matthew Taylor for lending invaluable insight and information.

Professor Gary White for his careful comments and helpful rewriting of the manuscript.

My wife, Akiko, and our daughter, Mai, for putting up with stacks of "junk" all over our three-room apartment and allowing me the latitude to finish the job.

A special thanks to all my ESL students at Sugiyama University, Nagoya, Japan, who offered suggestions and expressed their support for the educational benefits they derived from using this book as a pilot project, which resulted in overwhelmingly positive results.

HOW THIS BOOK IS ORGANIZED

1. All words are listed in alphabetical order by the *first* word only.
   Example: **ant / aunt** comes before **ate / eight**
2. All apostrophe words (conjunctions) are listed in alphabetical order regardless of apostrophe. The way you see it spelled is how it will be referred to in the text.
   Example: **their / there / they're**
3. Common names of people have been omitted for the sake of clarity.
   Example: you will *not* see Hart / Heart
   Mr. Hart had a heart attack.
4. All words are listed alphabetically in the back of the text for quick reference. The number after the word indicates the page on which the word, with definition, first appears.
5. The book is divided into Section One, Section Two, and Section Three. At the end of each section there is a word review containing many of the new words covered in that section. Answers to each review section along with a Comprehensive Review are in the back of the book right before the Index.
6. The words with an asterisk (*) are those words, or variations of words, that have already been learned in previous chapters. These words are also listed in a boxed area on the page. This constantly reinforces the definition and usage of the word. Repetition is a key method in this study manual.

For the sake of clarity and simplicity the asterisk is only used in the main body of the example sentences. Asterisks do not appear in the word definitions, **Note** Sections, Practice Exercises, and all Review Sections.

SECTION ONE

ad / add

Study these words to learn their differences.

1 **ad** – advertisement

a. That car **ad** is very good.
b. Did you see the new **ad** on the billboard?
c. I put an **ad** in the newspaper.

2 **add** – to join or unite

a. **Add** some thinner to the paint.
b. The coach wants to **add** a new member to the team.
c. I am going to **add** another room to my house.

3 **add** – plus (mathematics)

a. Subtract is the opposite of **add**.
b. In elementary school, students learn to **add**, subtract, multiply and divide.
c. What is the answer if you **add** five and nine?

PRACTICE EXERCISES

Write the correct word in the blank space. (Answers at bottom.)

1. The market ________________ was not very successful.
2. I forgot to ________________ sugar to the flour.
3. He never learned how to ________________ in elementary school.
4. The newspaper editor didn't like the ________________.
5. "You should ________________ more narrative," advised the teacher.

Write your own sentences.

1. ____
2. ____
3. ____

Answers: **1. ad 2. add 3. add 4. ad 5. add**

air / err / heir

Study these words to learn their differences.

*Previously Used Words
ad

1 **air** - a mixture of nitrogen and oxygen surrounding the earth

a. The rocket climbed high into the **air**.
b. **Air** in Los Angeles is sometimes very bad.
c. Mountain **air** is usually crisp and clear.

2 **air** - demeanor; attitude

a. She had the **air** of a rich person.
b. The student had an **air** of defiance.
c. His cocky **air** didn't impress anyone.

3 **air** - to express or say something

a. He didn't have a chance to **air** his opinion.
b. In communist countries it is very dangerous to **air** your personal feelings.
c. The mother wouldn't let her child **air** his ideas.

4 **air** - to send over the airwaves by radio, TV, or satellite

a. The director decided to **air** the program at night.
b. There wasn't enough money to **air** the ad*.
c. They will **air** the championship fight via satellite.

5 **err** - to make a mistake

a. To **err** is human.
b. He didn't **err** on his test.
c. The student was afraid she would **err** when she spoke.

6 **heir** - one who inherits something

a. She is the **heir** to her father's business.
b. His son was **heir** to the throne.
c. Mrs. Jones was the only **heir** in the will.

Practice Exercises on next page.

air / err / heir

PRACTICE EXERCISES

Write the correct word in the blank space. (Answers at bottom.)

1. Peter was the ________________ to a large fortune.
2. The ________________ in the room smelled awful.
3. If the man is not careful he will ________________ on the receipt.
4. Our president always tries to put on an ________________ of authority.
5. Management didn't want to ________________ the concert.

Write your own sentences.

1. ____
2. ____
3. ____
4. ____
5. ____
6. ____

Answers: 1. heir   2. air   3. err   4. air   5. air

aisle / I'll / isle

Study these words to learn their differences.

*Previously Used Words
ad

1 **aisle** - a walkway separating sections of seats in an auditorium, movie theater, sports arena, etc.

a. The bride and groom walked down the main **aisle** of the church.
b. The **aisle** in the old theater was very narrow.
c. We asked the usher to show us where our **aisle** was.

2 **I'll** - I will

a. "I don't want to, but **I'll** go," sighed Allen.
b. Do you think **I'll** pass the class?
c. "**I'll** never go out with him again!" declared Kathy.

3 **isle** - a small island

a. The **Isle** of Man is located between England and Ireland.
b. We sailed out to the **isle** for a picnic.
c. The ad* said the **isle** was uninhabited.

PRACTICE EXERCISES

Write the correct word in the blank space. (Answers at bottom.)

1. The theater ______________ was crowded with people.
2. He wants to live on a small ______________ in the Pacific.
3. ______________ go with you.
4. I like the window seat instead of the ______________ seat.
5. The water around the deserted ______________ was crystal clear.

Write your own sentences.

1. ____
2. ____
3. ____

Answers: 1. aisle 2. isle 3. I'll 4. aisle 5. isle

altar / alter

Study these words to learn their differences.

***Previously Used Words**
aisle

1 **altar** - a place where religious sacrifices are offered or incense is burned

a. The monk lit the incense on the **altar**.
b. Many religions used to offer animals on an **altar**.
c. They walked down the aisle* to the **altar**.

2 **alter** - to change

a. I had to **alter** my vacation plans because of the weather.
b. The councilman refused to **alter** his position.
c. World leaders try to **alter** the course of history.

PRACTICE EXERCISES

Write the correct word in the blank space. (Answers at bottom.)

1. The priest walked up to the ________________ with his head bowed.
2. Mr. Jones had to ________________ his suit because he lost weight.
3. The ancient ________________ was made of gold.
4. We had to ________________ our plans because of rain.
5. The bride and groom stood in front of the ________________.

Write your own sentences.

1. ____
2. ____

Answers: 1. altar 2. alter 3. altar 4. alter 5. altar

ant / aunt

Study these words to learn their differences.

*Previously Used Words
alter
heir

1 **ant** - a small insect with a complex social structure

a. An **ant** bite can hurt a lot.
b. My little sister screamed when she saw the **ant**.
c. The man put **ant** poison around his house.

2 **aunt** - the sister of a person's father or mother

a. My **aunt** decided to alter* her skirt instead of buying a new one.
b. Her **aunt** was the sole heir* to the fortune.
c. Their **aunt** and uncle always have a big Christmas party.

PRACTICE EXERCISES

Write the correct word in the blank space. (Answers at bottom.)

1. A red __________________ bit me on the foot.
2. His __________________ is very nice.
3. She is my favorite __________________.
4. The little boy had a small __________________ farm.
5. My __________________ came to visit last year.

Write your own sentences.

1. ____
2. ____

Answers: 1. ant 2. aunt 3. aunt 4. ant 5. aunt

ate / eight

Study these words to learn their differences.

***Previously Used Words**
aunt

1 **ate** – past tense of eat; to have eaten or consumed something

a. The tourist **ate** three hamburgers.
b. I think I **ate** too much.
c. The little girl **ate** the whole pizza.

2 **eight** – the number eight; 8

a. There are **eight** people in my aunt's* family.
b. The engine has **eight** cylinders.
c. **Eight** students were absent yesterday.

PRACTICE EXERCISES

✎ ***Write the correct word in the blank space. (Answers at bottom.)***

1. All ________________ men refused to enter the abandoned mine.
2. I ________________ all the cake.
3. They won't be back until ________________ o'clock.
4. The little boy ________________ too much and got sick.
5. There are ________________ drivers in the race.

✎ ***Write your own sentences.***

1. ____
2. ____

Answers: 1. eight 2. ate 3. eight 4. ate 5. eight

ball / bawl

Study these words to learn their differences.

***Previously Used Words**

air
aunt
ate

1 **ball** - a round or oval object used in games and sports

a. Bill hit the **ball** out of the park.
b. Their player kicked the **ball** high into the air*.
c. Every time I play golf I lose at least one **ball**.

2 **ball** - a large formal gathering or get-together

a. The masquerade **ball** was a lot of fun.
b. Linda was mad because she wasn't invited to the **ball**.
c. The graduation **ball** was a huge success.

3 **ball** - a good time

a. We had a **ball** last night.
b. The beach party was a real **ball**.
c. Everybody had a **ball** at the poker game.

4 **bawl** - to cry loudly

a. Spoiled children **bawl** very easily.
b. When his aunt* ate* the last piece of pie the child started to **bawl**.
c. The girl started to **bawl** when the doctor gave her a shot.

Note: The expression *bawl out* means to reprimand loudly or harshly. Example: The boss tends to *bawl out* new employees.

PRACTICE EXERCISES

Write the correct word in the blank space. (Answers at bottom.)

1. Every time he couldn't get his way the child would start to ________________.
2. There were many people at the ________________.
3. We had a ________________ at the party.
4. The little girl lost her balloon and started to ________________.
5. The receiver dropped the ________________ in the end zone.

Write your own sentences.

1. ____
2. ____
3. ____
4. ____

Answers: 1. bawl 2. ball 3. ball 4. bawl 5. ball

bare / bear

Study these words to learn their differences.

> ***Previously Used Words**
> ball

1 **bare** – lacking any type of covering; naked; nude

a. She caught the ball* with her **bare** hands.
b. The child had **bare** feet and no shirt.
c. His **bare** back got sunburned.

2 **bear** – a large heavy mammal with shaggy hair that eats meat, fruits, and insects

a. The grizzly **bear** is now an endangered species in North America.
b. Every **bear** in the zoo looked healthy.
c. I once saw a polar **bear** in Alaska.

3 **bear** – to carry something, physically or mentally

a. He had to **bear** the burden of being poor.
b. The camel had to **bear** the heavy load of wood.
c. The wounded soldier could hardly **bear** the pain.

PRACTICE EXERCISES

✎ *Write the correct word in the blank space. (Answers at bottom.)*

1. Some girls on Bondi Beach were ________________ from the waist up.
2. It was hard for him to ________________ the false statements.
3. The huge ________________ came wandering into our camp.
4. The small donkey couldn't ________________ the load.
5. I burned my ________________ feet on the hot pavement.

✎ *Write your own sentences.*

1. ____
2. ____
3. ____

Answers: 1. bare 2. bear 3. bear 4. bear 5. bare

base / bass

Study these words to learn their differences.

***Previously Used Words**
air
alter
bear

1 **base** - the bottom of something

a. The **base** of the lamp is metal.
b. All around the **base** of the mountain was covered with flowers.
c. I cracked the **base** of my computer.

2 **base** - a military installation

a. The residents do not want a military **base** near town.
b. The air* at the **base** of operations was almost black with smoke.
c. During the night the soldiers snuck three girls on **base**.

3 **base** - vile; mean

a. That lady is a very **base** individual.
b. His friend was advised to alter* his **base** attitude.
c. Some people think it is manly to be **base**.

4 **base** - any one of four safe areas on a baseball infield

a. The runner was out because he didn't touch second **base**.
b. The player tripped over the **base**.
c. Pete slid into third **base** safely.

5 **bass** - with a deep or low tone

a. His music teacher couldn't bear* to listen to him play the **bass** guitar.
b. The **bass** singer was very good.
c. I dropped the **bass** drum and broke the head.

Note: *Bass* is also a type of fish. The spelling is the same but the pronunciation is different with a short *a* sound, as in *pass*. Check your dictionary for proper usage.

Practice Exercises on next page.

base / bass

PRACTICE EXERCISES

Write the correct word in the blank space. (Answers at bottom.)

1. The ________________ of the table was broken.
2. There were many soldiers on the ________________.
3. He had a deep ________________ voice.
4. That man was very ________________ in his remarks.
5. It's a long throw from home plate to second ________________.

Write your own sentences.

1. ____
2. ____
3. ____
4. ____
5. ____

Answers: 1. base 2. base 3. bass 4. base 5. base

be / bee

Study these words to learn their differences.

*Previously Used Words
eight
altar

1 **be** - to have or maintain a place or position

a. He will **be** senator for eight* more months.
b. She will **be** champion for the next five years.
c. I will **be** here for about 10 more minutes.

2 **be** - to take place or occur

a. Our party will **be** this coming Saturday.
b. She is going to **be** our next president.
c. The new director will **be** here tomorrow.

3 **bee** - an insect that produces honey

a. A **bee** sting is very painful.
b. The **bee** flew in and landed on the altar*.
c. The buzzing **bee** scared everyone in the room.

PRACTICE EXERCISES

Write the correct word in the blank space. (Answers at bottom.)

1. Linda will ____________________ the chairperson of the committee.
2. We will ____________________ going to the beach next Saturday.
3. The ____________________ landed on my nose.
4. Will they ____________________ at the party?
5. A worker ____________________ collects nectar to make honey.

Write your own sentences.

1. ____
2. ____
3. ____

Answers: 1. be 2. be 3. bee 4. be 5. bee

beat / beet

Study these words to learn their differences.

*Previously Uscd Words
eight
bass
altar
aunt
bawl

1 **beat** - to strike or hit many times

a. Eight* people **beat** the man to death.
b. My wife **beat** the eggs then folded them into the batter.
c. The carpenter **beat** the nail into the wood.

2 **beat** - to win

a. We **beat** all the other teams.
b. I hope the Tigers **beat** the Giants.
c. The college team couldn't **beat** the pros.

3 **beat** - rhythm; tempo

a. Rock music usually has a hard-driving **beat** with a heavy bass* line.
b. When playing music, try not to miss a **beat**.
c. The **beat** was really fast.

4 **beat** - extremely tired; exhausted

a. He's too **beat** to walk to the altar*.
b. Since I didn't sleep last night I'm really **beat** today.
c. "I'm **beat**," declared my aunt*.

5 **beet** - a red garden plant used as a vegetable

a. A **beet** and onion salad is delicious.
b. The baby started to bawl* when he tasted the **beet** juice.
c. The last **beet** in the bag was rotten.

Note: *Beet red* is also used to describe someone who is very angry or embarrassed. Example: He turned *beet red* with anger. Example: She was so ashamed that she turned *beet red*.

Practice Exercises on next page.

beat / beet

PRACTICE EXERCISES

Write the correct word in the blank space. (Answers at bottom.)

1. Our team finally ______________ them.
2. The farmer put salt on the raw ______________ and ate it.
3. The song's ______________ was very slow.
4. Their whole group was ______________ from the long hike.
5. His horse ate both the ______________ and carrot.

Write your own sentences.

1. ______________________________
2. ______________________________
3. ______________________________
4. ______________________________
5. ______________________________

Answers: 1. beat 2. beet 3. beat 4. beat 5. beet

been / bin

Study these words to learn their differences.

***Previously Used Words**
bee
beet

1 **been** - past participle of be

a. I have never **been** stung by a bee*.
b. How long have you **been** here?
c. She has never **been** to Disneyland.

2 **bin** - a container used for storing or holding things

a. Throw the trash in the **bin**.
b. That metal **bin** is for glass only.
c. The clerk threw the beet* into the wrong **bin**.

PRACTICE EXERCISES

Write the correct word in the blank space. (Answers at bottom.)

1. A homeless person was sleeping in the ______________.
2. Have you ever ______________ to a foreign country?
3. Everybody has already ______________ to that movie.
4. The trash ______________ was full.
5. Every ______________ was made of plastic.

Write your own sentences.

1. ____
2. ____

Answers: 1. bin 2. been 3. been 4. bin 5. bin

berry / bury

Study these words to learn their differences.

*Previously Used Words
bear
been
base

1 **berry** - a small fruit

a. My favorite dessert is any kind of **berry** pie.
b. The bear* roamed through the **berry** patch.
c. Have you ever been* to Knott's **Berry** Farm?

2 **bury** - to put into the earth

a. Most Americans **bury** their dead instead of cremating them.
b. Pirates used to **bury** stolen treasure.
c. When our pet dog died we decided to **bury** it at the base* of the old oak tree.

PRACTICE EXERCISES

Write the correct word in the blank space. (Answers at bottom.)

1. I love to visit my uncle's __________________ farm.
2. My dog likes to __________________ all his bones.
3. Have you ever been __________________ picking?
4. The robbers decided not to __________________ the money.
5. He eats __________________ preserves with butter and toast every morning.

Write your own sentences.

1. ____
2. ____

Answers: 1. berry 2. bury 3. berry 4. bury 5. berry

berth / birth

Study these words to learn their differences.

***Previously Used Words**
berry
bawl
eight

1 **berth** - a place to sit or sleep usually on a ship or train

a. The **berth** we had was very comfortable.
b. Her young child spilled berry* juice in the train **berth** and then started to bawl*.
c. A first class **berth** is rather expensive.

2 **birth** - when a baby is born

a. She gave **birth** to a healthy eight* pound baby girl.
b. Do you have your **birth** certificate with you?
c. **Birth** control is a very controversial subject.

PRACTICE EXERCISES

Write the correct word in the blank space. (Answers at bottom.)

1. The ________________ in the train was too small.
2. Every ________________ on the ship was cheap.
3. Her ________________ was cause for celebration.
4. Many people have different opinions about ________________ control.
5. A first class ________________ costs $2,000.

Write your own sentences.

1. ____
2. ____

Answers: 1. berth 2. berth 3. birth 4. birth 5. berth

bi / buy / by / bye

Study these words to learn their differences.

***Previously Used Words**
bin
berth
ball

1 **bi** - two; two times

a. Both sides attended the **bi**lateral meeting.
b. My friend's Spanish teacher is **bi**lingual.
c. It's a **bi**weekly newspaper.

Note: In this case *bi* is a prefix, coming in front of the main or root word. A suffix comes at the end of a word. Example: remodeling—*re* is the prefix, *model* is the main or root word, and *ing* is the suffix.

Second Note: The word *biweekly* in example c can be confusing, because it can mean two times a week *or* every other week. To be precise it is better to say *every other week* or *two times a week*. You can also use *twice a week*. Similar words to be careful of are *bimonthly* and *biannually*.

2 **buy** - to purchase something

a. I'm going to **buy** a garbage bin*.
b. My sister wants to **buy** an economy class berth* on the ship.
c. I don't like to **buy** expensive jewelry.

3 **buy** - a good deal; a bargain

a. It was a great **buy**.
b. We got a pretty decent **buy** on our house.
c. They are having a good **buy** on apples today.

Note: The word *buy* can also be used to indicate belief or credibility. Example: I don't *buy* her reason for being late.

4 **by** - next to; near

a. He lives **by** the river.
b. The department store is **by** the station.
c. Her house is **by** the school.

5 **by** - past; to go past

a. The ball* went **by** him.
b. The car raced **by** the policeman.
c. Ben ran **by** his opponent in the last second.

6 **by** - something from someone or something

a. The song was written **by** her.
b. "I wonder who this painting is **by**?" asked the visitor.
c. *The Grapes of Wrath* was written **by** John Steinbeck.

7 **by** - used for measurement or for measuring something

a. The room size is six feet **by** nine feet.
b. Their new lot is fifty **by** one hundred feet.
c. Nine **by** 12 is the average size of an American carpet.

Note: Many times *by* is represented as ×. Example: The city block is 500 feet wide × 1000 feet long.

bi / buy / by / bye

8 **bye** - good-bye; farewell

a. "See you tomorrow, **bye**," called the mailman.
b. The girl waved **bye** to her father.
c. Many people in America simply say "**bye**" on the telephone.

Note: The word *good-bye* can also be spelled *good-by*. Also, *bye-bye* is often used.

PRACTICE EXERCISES

Write the correct word in the blank space. (Answers at bottom.)

1. The ________________ weekly newspaper sold very well.
2. I want to ________________ a new coat.
3. John called out, "________________," as he ran down the street.
4. She lives ________________ the old mansion.
5. The train went ________________ the station without stopping.

Write your own sentences.

1. ____
2. ____
3. ____
4. ____
5. ____
6. ____
7. ____
8. ____

Answers: 1. bi 2. buy 3. bye 4. by 5. by

blew / blue

Study these words to learn their differences.

*Previously Used Words
ant
beat
base

1 **blew** - past tense of blow; forced with air or wind

a. The girl **blew** out the candles on the birthday cake.
b. The wind **blew** an ant* onto the table.
c. My father **blew** up the balloon.

2 **blew** - made a mistake; blundered

a. I **blew** the final examination.
b. He **blew** the deal because he beat* the desk with his fist.
c. My error at first base* **blew** the whole game.

Note: This usage is considered slang.

3 **blue** - the color blue

a. She gave birth to a boy, so we bought him tiny **blue** socks.
b. White clouds dotted the **blue** sky.
c. My niece's favorite color is **blue**.

PRACTICE EXERCISES

Write the correct word in the blank space. (Answers at bottom.)

1. Diane was embarrassed when her husband ________________ his nose in church.
2. I ________________ my chance when I failed the final oral examination.
3. In Perth, Australia, the sky is ________________ almost everyday.
4. They ________________ out the candles together.
5. Both the American and French flags are red, white, and ________________.

Write your own sentences.

1. ____
2. ____
3. ____

Answers: 1. blew 2. blew 3. blue 4. blew 5. blue

boar / bore

Study these words to learn their differences.

*Previously Used Words
bear

1 **boar** - a wild pig

a. A **boar** is extremely dangerous.
b. **Boar** meat is very good to eat.
c. The **boar** chased the bear* into the woods.

2 **bore** - to cut with a twisting movement to make a hole

a. The heavy drill **bore** through the rocks.
b. The workman began to **bore** a hole in the metal.
c. We decided to **bore** a hole in the wall.

3 **bore** - not interesting; dull

a. The speaker was a total **bore**.
b. He is a real **bore** to talk to.
c. "I have never met such a **bore**," complained Sally.

PRACTICE EXERCISES

Write the correct word in the blank space. (Answers at bottom.)

1. The ________________ started to run after the hunter.
2. He tried to ________________ a hole into the concrete.
3. It is such a ________________ to visit with them.
4. The carpenter ________________ two holes in the piece of wood.
5. "Why are statistics classes such a ________________?" complained Carl.

Write your own sentences.

1. ____
2. ____
3. ____

Answers: 1. boar 2. bore 3. bore 4. bore 5. bore

board / bored

Study these words to learn their differences.

1 **board** - a piece of sawed wood with its length much longer than its width

a. She used a **board** to fix the fence.
b. The carpenter cut the **board** in half.
c. The black walnut **board** was very expensive.

2 **board** - to provide daily meals usually for pay

a. The job didn't include **board**.
b. Mrs. Smith's **board** was always delicious.
c. **Board** was included for all the students.

Note: Many times *board* is used together with ***room and board***, which means a place to live with meals included.

3 **board** - a group of people with certain powers

a. The education **board** decided all the school rules.
b. Our **board** of directors voted to raise their pay.
c. The **board** of examiners meets once a month.

4 **bored** - past tense of bore; not interesting; dull

a. I was **bored** by his constant bragging.
b. She was very **bored** during the holiday break.
c. Every student in class seemed **bored**.

PRACTICE EXERCISES

✎ *Write the correct word in the blank space. (Answers at bottom.)*

1. The members of the ________________ were all present.
2. He was ________________ at the party.
3. Room and ________________ were both included in the new job offer.
4. The director of the ________________ decided to resign.
5. The electrician ________________ a hole in the concrete.

✎ *Write your own sentences.*

1. ____
2. ____
3. ____
4. ____

Answers: 1. board 2. bored 3. board 4. board 5. bored

brake / break

Study these words to learn their differences.

*Previously Used Words
base blue

1 **brake** - something used to slow down or stop motion or movement

a. When you park your car remember to apply the hand **brake**.
b. My truck's emergency **brake** needs to be repaired.
c. The parking **brake** wasn't adjusted properly.

Note: *Hand brake, emergency brake,* and *parking brake* can all be used to mean the same thing.

2 **break** - to suddenly separate into parts

a. Fragile things **break** easily.
b. She was careful not to **break** the base* of the blue* antique lamp.
c. They were afraid to **break** up their marriage.

3 **break** - a short rest

a. "Let's take a **break**," suggested the chairperson.
b. Most companies have a 15-minute **break** twice a day.
c. Everyone wanted to take a short coffee **break**.

4 **break** - luck; good luck or bad luck

a. It was a tough **break** to lose the race.
b. Winning the lottery was the luckiest **break** in his life.
c. Musicians are always looking for their first big **break**.

Note: This usage is considered idiomatic.

Practice Exercises on next page.

brake / break

PRACTICE EXERCISES

Write the correct word in the blank space. (Answers at bottom.)

1. I hope their marriage doesn't ____________________ up.
2. She applied the ____________________ at just the right time.
3. Let's take a 10-minute ____________________.
4. Paul got a ____________________ to try out for the team.
5. The ____________________ on the train was faulty.

Write your own sentences.

1. ____
2. ____
3. ____
4. ____

Answers: 1. break 2. brake 3. break 4. break 5. brake

bread / bred

Study these words to learn their differences.

1 **bread** - baked and leavened food made of flour, meal, and water

a. Whole wheat **bread** is good for your health.
b. Chinese eat more rice than **bread**.
c. Our bakery makes really delicious **bread**.

2 **bread** - money

a. I lost all my **bread** playing poker.
b. "Can I borrow some **bread**?" asked the poor looking man.
c. He's all out of **bread**.

Note: This usage is considered slang.

3 **bred** - past tense of breed; produced or propagated (plants or animals)

a. Many champion horses have been **bred** on farms in Kentucky.
b. The scientists **bred** a stronger type of corn.
c. It is a good idea to have pedigree animals **bred** from a long distance, to prevent crossbreeding.

PRACTICE EXERCISES

Write the correct word in the blank space. (Answers at bottom.)

1. Mr. Thompson's race horse was ________________ in England.
2. We don't have any ________________ or milk.
3. The day old ________________ was a very good buy.
4. I don't have enough ________________ for a new car.
5. The beautiful flower was ________________ from two different varieties.

Write your own sentences.

1. ____
2. ____
3. ____

Answers: 1. bred 2. bread 3. bread 4. bread 5. bred

capital / capitol

Study these words to learn their differences.

***Previously Used Words**

blew
blue

1 **capital** - punishable by death

a. In many countries murder is a **capital** offense.
b. Most people are outraged by **capital** crimes.
c. "Do you think **capital** punishment is a good idea?" asked the professor.

2 **capital** - value of all goods

a. The company's **capital** is over $10,000,000.
b. All my **capital** is tied up in real estate.
c. His family has a large amount of **capital**.

3 **capital** - upper case letter; large letter

a. This is a **capital** C.
b. Always spell a person's name beginning with a **capital**.
c. The secretary forgot to make the initial with a **capital** letter.

Note: *X, Y, Z,* are *capital, upper case* or *large letters,* whereas *a, b, c* are *lower case* or *small letters.*

4 **capital** - a city serving as the seat of government

a. Tokyo is the **capital** of Japan.
b. "Paris is the most beautiful **capital** in the world," declared the Frenchman.
c. Do you know the population of the **capital**?

5 **capitol** - a group of buildings in which government functions are performed

a. The California state **capitol** building is located in Sacramento.
b. The wind blew* leaves down the **capitol** steps.
c. The state **capitol** building's roof is painted blue* and has large white pillars in front.

Note: The words *Capitol Hill* mean the legislative branch of the United States government. Example: The rumors about the scandal began on *Capitol Hill*.

Practice Exercises on next page.

capital / capitol

PRACTICE EXERCISES

Write the correct word in the blank space. (Answers at bottom.)

1. The developing country's ________________ was very low.
2. Some poets refuse to use ________________ letters.
3. Do you believe in ________________ punishment?
4. Wellington is the ________________ of New Zealand.
5. The ________________ building was modern in design.

Write your own sentences.

1. ____
2. ____
3. ____
4. ____
5. ____

Answers: 1. capital 2. capital 3. capital 4. capital 5. capitol

cell / sell

Study these words to learn their differences.

*Previously Used Words
bare
boar
buy
aunt

1 **cell** - a small room or compartment

a. The prisoner was confined to a **cell**.
b. The walls in the **cell** were bare*.
c. The boar* cage was nothing more than a small square **cell**.

2 **cell** - a very small mass of protoplasm

a. All the doctors examined the cancer **cell** under a microscope.
b. I never liked studying **cell** structure.
c. The instructor had us draw a picture of a **cell**.

3 **sell** - to give something for money

a. I'm going to **sell** my house next year.
b. The opposite of **sell** is buy*.
c. "Why don't you **sell** your bike instead of throwing it away?" asked the boy's aunt*.

PRACTICE EXERCISES

Write the correct word in the blank space. (Answers at bottom.)

1. The animal was locked in a small ________________.
2. All the students watched as the ________________ began to divide.
3. It is not easy to ________________ a used car.
4. Under the microscope the ________________ appeared to be abnormal.
5. A good salesperson must ________________ many products.

Write your own sentences.

1. ____
2. ____
3. ____

Answers: 1. cell 2. cell 3. sell 4. cell 5. sell

censor / sensor

Study these words to learn their differences.

*Previously Used Words
cell

1 **censor** - an official or government body that examines all types of material for objectionable matter; to alter according to law

a. The government decided to **censor** the movie.
b. A **censor** reviews all Japanese education textbooks.
c. In many countries a **censor** is very powerful.

2 **sensor** - a device that responds to stimuli and in turn sends an impulse

a. A pacemaker is a small **sensor** that helps the heart to function properly.
b. My car has a police **sensor** in it.
c. The scientist probed the cell* with an electric **sensor**.

PRACTICE EXERCISES

Write the correct word in the blank space. (Answers at bottom.)

1. The ________________ took out all the bad words in the book.
2. Her computer diagram helped to develop the new ________________.
3. The author and the ________________ got into an argument.
4. I had to buy a new ________________ for my portable telephone.
5. The government ________________ tried to completely change the book.

Write your own sentences.

1. ____
2. ____

Answers: 1. censor 2. sensor 3. censor 4. sensor 5. censor

cent / scent / sent

Study these words to learn their differences.

*Previously Used Words
boar
blue
by

1 **cent** - the smallest monetary unit of the United States

a. In America, one **cent** is often called a penny.
b. "One more **cent**, please," said the cashier.
c. When I was young I could buy candy for one **cent** each.

2 **scent** - smell; odor; fragrance

a. A skunk has a very strong **scent**.
b. The **scent** of her perfume lingered in the room.
c. The hound tried to pick up the **scent** of the boar*.

3 **sent** - past and past participle of send; to have posted a card, letter, package, etc.

a. I **sent** my mother a beautiful blue* Christmas card.
b. They **sent** me a package for my birthday.
c. She **sent** all the information by* fax.

Note: *Fax* is short for *facsimile*.

PRACTICE EXERCISES.

Write the correct word in the blank space. (Answers at bottom.)

1. The miser counted every ________________ he had three times every night.
2. His after shave lotion had a very strong ________________.
3. I ________________ the letter yesterday.
4. You could smell the ________________ of cut hay in the air.
5. The child was happy that he found one ________________ on the ground.

Write your own sentences.

1. ____
2. ____
3. ____

Answers: 1. cent 2. scent 3. sent 4. scent 5. cent

cents / sense / scents

Study these words to learn their differences.

*Previously Used Words
eight

1 **cents** - plural of cent; the smallest monetary units of the United States

a. "That candy bar costs 50 **cents**," said the clerk.
b. Most Americans say 10 **cents**, not 10 pennies.
c. It only costs eight* cents a day for my car insurance.

2 **sense** - of, or regarding, the organs of sight, hearing, smell, taste, or touch

a. When a kitten is born its **sense** of sight is very poor.
b. A dog's **sense** of hearing is keen.
c. The **sense** of smell and taste is important for a chef.

3 **sense** - a kind of feeling, sensation or awareness

a. Although the dancer was big he had a delicate **sense** of balance.
b. You could **sense** the president's insecurity every time he spoke.
c. A **sense** of guilt overcame the deserter.

4 **sense** - showing intelligence or sound mental capacity; ability to make good judgments

a. Her decision to cancel the contract showed good **sense**.
b. That idea doesn't make any **sense** at all.
c. "What's the **sense** of raising taxes?" asked the reporter.

Note: *Sense* means a reliable ability to make decisions with sound intelligence. *Common sense* means an average ability to make decisions or to know the basics of something without any special training or knowledge.

5 **scents** - plural of scent; smells, odors, fragrances

a. The different **scents** of the escaped convicts were easy for the dogs to discern.
b. After awhile all the **scents** of the herbs smelled the same.
c. The makeup consultant had a special description for all the **scents** of perfume that were for sale.

Practice Exercises on next page.

PRACTICE EXERCISES

Write the correct word in the blank space. (Answers at bottom.)

1. The director's decision showed good ________________.

2. I only have six ________________ left.

3. Bob could always ________________ when there was trouble.

4. His ________________ of hearing is very poor.

5. The different ________________ of flowers filled the little shop.

Write your own sentences.

1. ____

2. ____

3. ____

4. ____

5. ____

Answers: **1. sense 2. cents 3. sense 4. sense 5. scents**

cereal / serial

Study these words to learn their differences.

*Previously Used Words
ate

1 **cereal** - made of grain and usually eaten with milk and sugar for breakfast

a. When she was here she ate* **cereal** every morning.
b. Many Americans have **cereal** for breakfast.
c. Cornflakes are my favorite **cereal**.

2 **serial** - arranged in order or progression

a. **Serial** numbers on paper money make it easy to trace.
b. The thief changed the **serial** number on the car engine.
c. Flash Gordon was a popular television **serial**.

Note: Example c is now usually referred to as a *series* instead of a *serial*. Example: "The Fugitive" was a TV *series* in America about 25 years ago.

PRACTICE EXERCISES

Write the correct word in the blank space. (Answers at bottom.)

1. My sister eats ________________ every morning.
2. Many soap operas are in ________________ form.
3. The ________________ number on the radio was easy to read.
4. I like dry ________________ the best.
5. Bananas and cream taste great on ________________.

Write your own sentences.

1. ____
2. ____

Answers: 1. cereal 2. serial 3. serial 4. cereal 5. cereal

cite / sight / site

*Previously Used Words
scent
bread
capital

Study these words to learn their differences.

1 **cite** - to quote an example

a. Professor Jones wants me to **cite** all my references.
b. The guest speaker tended to **cite** very difficult sources.
c. A good research paper will **cite** many different authors.

2 **sight** - having to do with the eyes

a. The old man's **sight** is not very good.
b. I think my **sight** is getting worse.
c. When babies are first born their **sight** is very poor.

3 **sight** - something that can be seen

a. His train slowly came into **sight**.
b. The **sight** and scent* of newly baked bread* makes me hungry.
c. The watchful mother always kept her young child in **sight**.

4 **site** - place or location

a. Bill's construction **site** is located in the capital*.
b. The **site** for the new store was not a good choice.
c. The **site** of the eagle's nest was high on the mountain.

PRACTICE EXERCISES

Write the correct word in the blank space. (Answers at bottom.)

1. The lazy student failed to ________________ a single source.
2. Our new school ________________ is out in the country.
3. Jack hit the ball out of ________________.
4. Her ________________ is perfect.
5. Everyone agreed on the new building ________________.

Write your own sentences.

1. ____
2. ____
3. ____
4. ____

Answers: 1. cite 2. site 3. sight 4. sight 5. site

coarse / course

Study these words to learn their differences.

***Previously Used Words**
bore
air
site
capitol

1 **coarse** – crude in manner or language

a. "Not only is he a bore,* he is also very **coarse**," stated the lady, with an air* of authority.
b. Their way of acting is sometimes **coarse**.
c. The football coach always talks in a **coarse** manner.

2 **course** – a path over which something or someone moves

a. The **course** of his travels took him all over Europe.
b. That cross country **course** passed the new building site*.
c. The **course** through the woods led to the capitol* building's back door.

3 **course** – golf course

a. The **course** at Pebble Beach is extremely difficult.
b. It was only a nine hole **course**.
c. I can never get below 90 on that **course**.

Note: There are a number of other uses of the word *course* with a word or words added to it. *Off course* means to not be going in the right direction. Example: The ship is *off course*. *On course* means to be going in the right direction. Example: My son is *on course* in his college studies. *Par for the course* means something that is to be expected. Example: It was *par for the course* when John didn't get the contract. *Of course* means for sure or without a doubt. Example: *Of course* I like hamburgers. However, be aware that *of course* can sometimes have negative connotations, so be careful when using it. Example: "*Of course* I like her! " The intonation in this answer could imply, "Do you take me for a fool?" When in doubt it is better just to answer *yes* or *no*.

PRACTICE EXERCISES

Write the correct word in the blank space. (Answers at bottom.)

1. His ________________ manner of speaking was not appreciated.
2. The ________________ she took this summer was interesting.
3. The country club's new ________________ was very well planned.
4. John's survival ________________ was very rugged.
5. A ________________ attitude does not help good communication.

Write your own sentences.

1. ____
2. ____
3. ____

Answers: 1. coarse 2. course 3. course 4. course 5. coarse

dam / damn

Study these words to learn their differences.

1 **dam** - a body of water held behind a barrier

a. Hoover **Dam** is the biggest in America.
b. They took a break* and ate* cereal at the base* of the **dam**.
c. It took eight* years to build the **dam**.

2 **damn** - to swear; curse

a. "**Damn** it!" cursed the angry man.
b. He is a **damn** fool.
c. "That person doesn't know a **damn** thing!" exclaimed the angry citizen.

Note: This usage is considered coarse and should be avoided. However, *damn* is often used by native speakers to emphasize a point or idea. Its impact is more effective when used only on special occasions.

***Previously Used Words**
break
ate
base
eight

PRACTICE EXERCISES

Write the correct word in the blank space. (Answers at bottom.)

1. It takes many years to build a ________________.
2. "That's a ________________ stupid idea," blurted the angry stockholder.
3. We had a picnic by the ________________.
4. The new ________________ helped to generate much more electricity.
5. "Stop that right now, ________________ it," yelled the boss.

Write your own sentences.

1. ____
2. ____

Answers: 1. dam 2. damn 3. dam 4. dam 5. damn

dear / deer

Study these words to learn their differences.

1. **dear** – affectionate; fond

   a. They are very **dear** friends.
   b. His home country is very **dear** to him.
   c. Usually, when Americans start a letter, they begin by writing, **Dear**…

2. **dear** – a loved one

   a. Some American couples refer to each other as "**dear**."
   b. Her **dear** friend just passed away.
   c. She is very **dear** to me.

3. **deer** – an animal of the Cervidae family

   a. Canada has a lot of **deer**.
   b. All the **deer** in the park are gone.
   c. **Deer** meat is called "venison."

   Note: The plural of *deer* can be either *deer* or *deers*.

PRACTICE EXERCISES

Write the correct word in the blank space. (Answers at bottom.)

1. There was a ________________ standing right in the middle of the road.
2. Her mother's ________________ friend came to visit last weekend.
3. Many people are against ________________ hunting.
4. My neighbor always calls his wife ________________.
5. The famous hunter had a ________________ head mounted on his den wall.

Write your own sentences.

1. ____
2. ____
3. ____

Answers: 1. deer 2. dear 3. deer 4. dear 5. deer

desert / dessert

Study these words to learn their differences.

*Previously Used Words
base
course
censor

1 **desert** – to leave with no intention of returning; to run away; to abandon

a. Fair weather friends will **desert** you when the going gets tough.
b. The irate husband threatened to **desert** his wife.
c. The soldiers decided to **desert** their base* camp.

Note: By changing the pronunciation of the above word you have a completely different word, meaning a dry, arid place or area. Example: The Sahara is the biggest *desert* in the world. The spelling remains the same. Check your dictionary for details.

2 **dessert** – the last course of a meal; a sweet dish

a. The seven course* meal included **dessert**.
b. The censor* didn't want any **dessert**.
c. My sister's favorite **dessert** is apple pie.

PRACTICE EXERCISES

Write the correct word in the blank space. (Answers at bottom.)

1. He usually doesn't eat ________________.
2. Fred decided to ________________ his friends.
3. The ________________ was very fattening.
4. If you ________________ the army you can get into a lot of trouble.
5. My grandmother always serves a big ________________.

Write your own sentences.

1. ________________________________
2. ________________________________

Answers: 1. dessert 2. desert 3. dessert 4. desert 5. dessert

dew / do / due

Study these words to learn their differences.

1 **dew** - condensed moisture that usually forms at night

a. This morning there was **dew** on the lawn.
b. **Dew** was on all the windows.
c. In the early evening **dew** covered the flowers.

2 **do** - to bring to pass; perform

a. Good students always **do** their homework.
b. Make sure you **do** a good job.
c. The boy would not **do** as he was told.

3 **due** - something owed as a debt

a. Rent is **due** on the first of every month.
b. My car payment is past **due**.
c. When a bill comes **due** you should pay it on time.

PRACTICE EXERCISES

Write the correct word in the blank space. (Answers at bottom.)

1. The ________________ sparkled like diamonds in the morning sun.
2. "I'm ready to ________________ my part," declared the volunteer.
3. There is still a lot of money ________________ on my mortgage.
4. A light coat of ________________ covered the leaves.
5. I can ________________ the job in two weeks.

Write your own sentences.

1. ____
2. ____
3. ____

Answers: 1. dew 2. do 3. due 4. dew 5. do

doe / dough

Study these words to learn their differences.

1 **doe** – an adult female deer

a. A **doe** does not have antlers.
b. We saw a **doe** in the forest.
c. The **doe** ate* the corn in our garden.

Note: A male deer is called a *buck*. A baby deer is called a *fawn*.

2 **dough** – a mixture of flour and water that is made into bread

a. The baker kneaded the **dough** with his hands.
b. When I was a child I used to like to eat **dough**.
c. The chef put the **dough** into a bread* pan.

***Previously Used Words**

ate
bread

PRACTICE EXERCISES

Write the correct word in the blank space. (Answers at bottom.)

1. She kept the __________________ as a pet.
2. He mixed flour and water to make __________________.
3. A __________________ stood in the middle of the road.
4. The cook rolled the __________________ with a rolling pin.
5. A fly got stuck in the __________________.

Write your own sentences.

1. ____
2. ____

Answers: 1. doe 2. dough 3. doe 4. dough 5. dough

SECTION ONE WORD REVIEW

Part A

DIRECTIONS: *Here are some of the new words covered in Section One. Circle the one that fits best.*

1. My car payment is two months past (dew, do, due).
2. The music (beat, beet) was very fast.
3. A lone (dear, deer) stood in the middle of the road.
4. They threw the trash in the (been, bin).
5. He doesn't do a (damn, dam) thing right.
6. We decided to (berry, bury) the dead animal.
7. The (coarse, course) talking man embarrassed all his friends.
8. Our new home (cite, sight, site) is really beautiful.
9. I eat (cereal, serial) every morning for breakfast.
10. The (berth, birth) she slept in was too small.
11. My (aunt, ant) is very attractive.
12. His dog couldn't pick up the (cent, scent, sent) of the animal.
13. The (censor, sensor) checked the book very carefully.
14. His tendency to (heir, air, err) in fielding cost them the game.
15. During the recession Mrs. Johnson couldn't (cell, sell) her home.
16. The (capital, capitol) of Italy is Rome.
17. That television (ad, add) was very good.
18. It was hard to (bare, bear) the disappointment.
19. He had a beautiful (base, bass) voice.
20. The tailor will (altar, alter) my pants for free.

SECTION ONE WORD REVIEW

Part B

DIRECTIONS: *Match the words with their definitions. Write the letter in front of the word.*

____	1. bread	a. not interesting; dull
____	2. bee	b. good deal; bargain
____	3. ate	c. last course of a meal; a sweet dish
____	4. capital	d. next to
____	5. do	e. container used for holding things
____	6. bore	f. a body of water held behind a barrier
____	7. dear	g. smell
____	8. dessert	h. an insect that produces honey
____	9. bawl	i. money
____	10. isle	j. to run away; to abandon
____	11. dam	k. to bring to pass; to perform
____	12. break	l. a loved one
____	13. buy	m. to have eaten or consumed something
____	14. bin	n. to cry loudly
____	15. desert	o. made a mistake
____	16. by	p. large letter
____	17. due	q. a short rest
____	18. scent	r. small island
____	19. site	s. owing as a debt
____	20. blew	t. place or location

SECTION ONE WORD REVIEW

Part C

DIRECTIONS: *Circle Right or Wrong for the proper usage of each bold word in the following sentences.*

1. The members of the **bored** voted against the idea. Right / Wrong
2. The baker kneaded the **doe** into bread. Right / Wrong
3. He tried to **ad** some water to the paint. Right / Wrong
4. The girl stepped on the **ant**. Right / Wrong
5. My mother's **desert** was chocolate cake. Right / Wrong
6. What do you think of the new building **cite**? Right / Wrong
7. Her brother likes white **bread**. Right / Wrong
8. Local hunters shot the **boar**. Right / Wrong
9. His **coarse** behavior was not appreciated. Right / Wrong
10. Their house is **buy** the train station. Right / Wrong
11. The company **sent** the letter yesterday. Right / Wrong
12. Every trash **bin** was full. Right / Wrong
13. An early morning wind **blew** away the fog. Right / Wrong
14. The **break** on the motorcycle didn't work. Right / Wrong
15. I decided to **sell** my old typewriter. Right / Wrong
16. He **beet** the boy with a stick. Right / Wrong
17. John couldn't **bear** the thought of failing the test. Right / Wrong
18. She showed good **sense** by not arguing. Right / Wrong
19. The **capital** of Mexico is Mexico City. Right / Wrong
20. Her new computerized **sensor** was amazing. Right / Wrong

SECTION TWO

fair / fare

Study these words to learn their differences.

*Previously Used Words
due
coarse
site
ate
dessert
cite

1 **fair** - impartial; honest

a. He is a very **fair** businessman.
b. The judge tried to be **fair** about the money due* the plaintiff.
c. She was not **fair** in her decision because she didn't like the coarse* man's attitude.

2 **fair** - conforming to rules

a. In baseball, if the ball is not hit in **fair** ground, it is considered a foul ball.
b. It is not **fair** to hit below the belt in boxing.
c. The tennis match was **fair** since it was held at a neutral site*.

3 **fair** - a place where buyers and sellers gather at a set time for trade

a. I used to go to the county **fair** every year.
b. We ate* homemade dessert* when we went to the **fair**.
c. They had a big auction at the **fair**.

4 **fare** - a price charged for transportation

a. Air **fare** from Japan to America is not cheap.
b. The taxi **fare** was very expensive.
c. Our travel agent didn't cite* the correct **fare**.

Practice Exercises on next page.

fair / fare

PRACTICE EXERCISES

Write the correct word in the blank space. (Answers at bottom.)

1. The elderly couple didn't get a ________________ deal.
2. Neither team played ________________.
3. Both companies air ________________ was too expensive.
4. There were many rides at the ________________.
5. The bus ________________ was very reasonable.

Write your own sentences.

1. ____
2. ____
3. ____
4. ____

Answers: 1. fair 2. fair 3. fare 4. fair 5. fare

fairy / ferry

Study these words to learn their differences.

*Previously Used Words
heir

1 **fairy** - a mythical person with magical powers

a. Tinkerbelle was the name of the **fairy** in *Peter Pan*.
b. When American children are young they believe in the tooth **fairy**.
c. There was a **fairy** in the story.

2 **ferry** - to carry people or goods over land, sea, or air

a. They decided to **ferry** the troops by ship.
b. The plan to **ferry** the milk by train would take too long.
c. Our president ordered the airlines to **ferry** the starving people to hospitals.

3 **ferry** - a vehicle in which people or goods are carried across water or land in a boat, ship, or airplane; an organization or company that moves people or goods

a. We took the **ferry** for a sea cruise.
b. The captain made an error and the **ferry** hit another ship.
c. His partner was heir* to the entire **ferry** company.

PRACTICE EXERCISES

Write the correct word in the blank space. (Answers at bottom.)

1. The captain didn't want to ________________ the refugees back to sea.
2. In the story the ________________ saved all the children.
3. The ________________ sank in the rough seas.
4. Her two brothers wanted to start a ________________ company.
5. They used trucks to ________________ all the supplies.

Write your own sentences.

1. ____
2. ____
3. ____

Answers: 1. ferry 2. fairy 3. ferry 4. ferry 5. ferry

feat / feet

Study these words to learn their differences.

*Previously Used Words
bare

1 **feat** - a notable thing to do

a. When Charles Lindbergh first crossed the Atlantic it was considered a major aviation **feat**.
b. It was a major international **feat** when he ended the war.
c. Her book was a literary **feat**.

2 **feet** - plural of foot; the ends of legs upon which a person or animal stands

a. Many people walk on the beach in their bare* **feet**.
b. Ducks have strange looking **feet**.
c. His **feet** are very big.

PRACTICE EXERCISES

✎ *Write the correct word in the blank space. (Answers at bottom.)*

1. My ________________ hurt after standing all day.
2. The new shoes were tight on her ________________.
3. Janet's record breaking run was a track and field ________________.
4. It is not polite to put your ________________ up on a table.
5. The meeting was considered a major diplomatic ________________.

✎ *Write your own sentences.*

1. ____
2. ____

Answers: 1. feet 2. feet 3. feat 4. feet 5. feat

fir / fur

Study these words to learn their differences.

*Previously Used Words
dew
buy
desert

1 **fir** – an evergreen tree of the pine family

a. One of the most common trees in California is the Douglas **Fir**.
b. Dew* covered the huge **fir** tree.
c. Many houses are built of **fir**.

2 **fur** – the hairy coat of a mammal

a. His wife wants to buy* a **fur** coat.
b. The animal's **fur** was wet and matted.
c. The selfish man decided to desert* his family because his **fur** company went bankrupt.

PRACTICE EXERCISES

Write the correct word in the blank space. (Answers at bottom.)

1. We planted 100 ________________ trees in the forest.
2. The man was wearing a thick ________________ coat.
3. His dog's wet ________________ smelled terrible.
4. They decorated the ________________ in front of their house for Christmas.
5. The timber industry clear-cut all the ________________ in the area.

Write your own sentences.

1. ____
2. ____

Answers: **1. fir 2. fur 3. fur 4. fir 5. fir**

flair / flare

Study these words to learn their differences.

*Previously Used Words
ferry

1 **flair** - instinctive ability; talent

a. They both have a **flair** for good style.
b. Her **flair** for acting is phenomenal.
c. My husband has no **flair** for business.

2 **flair** - tendency

a. She has a **flair** for the melodramatic.
b. That agent has a **flair** to lie a lot.
c. Some people have a **flair** for stealing.

3 **flare** - to shine with sudden light

a. The forest fire began to **flare** in the night.
b. The sky over the city began to **flare** as bombs exploded.
c. The campfire started to **flare** in the dark forest.

4 **flare** - to become suddenly angry or upset

a. The boy began to **flare** up at the clerk.
b. Her boss started to **flare** up at the poor sales reports.
c. "Please don't **flare** up when I tell you the bad news," begged the woman.

Note: In this instance *flare* is usually used with *up*.

5 **flare** - a bright light or flame used as a signal

a. "Do you want me to light a **flare**?" asked a sailor on the ferry.*
b. The careless man stepped on the **flare**.
c. After the accident the driver set a **flare** on the road.

Practice Exercises on next page.

flair / flare

PRACTICE EXERCISES

Write the correct word in the blank space. (Answers at bottom.)

1. The emergency ________________ lit up the night sky.
2. He has a ________________ for being lazy.
3. The group began to ________________ up as the union leader spoke.
4. She has a ________________ for making ceramics.
5. The ________________ of the match startled everybody in the dark room.

Write your own sentences.

1. ____
2. ____
3. ____
4. ____
5. ____

Answers: 1. flare 2. flair 3. flare 4. flair 5. flare

flea / flee

Study these words to learn their differences.

***Previously Used Words**
site

1 **flea** - bloodsucking insect that feeds on warm-blooded animals

a. I bought some **flea** powder for my dog.
b. The scientist took many pictures of the **flea**.
c. A **flea** is a parasite.

2 **flee** - to run away from danger

a. The demonstrators vowed not to **flee** the site*.
b. After the hold-up the robber tried to **flee**.
c. A coward will **flee** in the face of danger.

PRACTICE EXERCISES

Write the correct word in the blank space. (Answers at bottom.)

1. The prisoner tried to ____________________ his captors.
2. I saw a ____________________ jump off the dog's back.
3. He stepped on the ____________________ with his boot.
4. They had no choice but to ____________________ the burning building.
5. The cornered fox couldn't ____________________ the approaching hunters.

Write your own sentences.

1. ____
2. ____

Answers: 1. flee 2. flea 3. flea 4. flee 5. flee

flew / flu / flue

Study these words to learn their differences.

*Previously Used Words
fare
isle
sight
bear

1 **flew** - past tense of fly; to move through the air

a. We **flew** to New York on a cut-rate fare*.
b. As they **flew** over the isle* they caught sight* of a black bear*.
c. Their father always **flew** business class.

2 **flu** - influenza

a. Everyone had the **flu** and was absent from school.
b. I had the **flu** for two weeks.
c. The **flu** made him weak and dizzy.

3 **flue** - an enclosed passageway for things like smoke and gas to pass through

a. Smoke from the small fire went up the **flue**.
b. Make sure the **flue** is open.
c. He cleaned the **flue** with a long chain.

PRACTICE EXERCISES

Write the correct word in the blank space. (Answers at bottom.)

1. Cleaning out the ________________ was a dirty job.
2. I haven't had the ________________ for five years.
3. The jet ________________ over the crowd of people.
4. Many people used to get a ________________ shot every year.
5. Her parakeet ________________ out the open window.

Write your own sentences.

1. ____
2. ____
3. ____

Answers: 1. flue 2. flu 3. flew 4. flu 5. flew

flour / flower

Study these words to learn their differences.

***Previously Used Words**
bear

1 **flour** – finely ground meal of wheat

a. She used white **flour** when she made the cake.
b. **Flour** in America is very cheap.
c. The heavy bag of **flour** was too much for the girl to bear*.

2 **flower** – the part of the plant used for reproduction

a. The bride had a single white **flower** in her hair.
b. On Valentine's Day he gave her a red **flower**.
c. My mother's favorite **flower** is a carnation.

PRACTICE EXERCISES

Write the correct word in the blank space. (Answers at bottom.)

1. The ________________ in the vase was purple.
2. The bag of ________________ was on sale.
3. There wasn't a single ________________ in the garden.
4. Our baker uses a special kind of ________________ for her bread.
5. The recipe called for three cups of ________________.

Write your own sentences.

1. ____
2. ____

Answers: 1. flower 2. flour 3. flower 4. flour 5. flour

for / fore / four

Study these words to learn their differences.

1 **for** - used to indicate purpose

a. She received a grant **for** studying how to reduce the birth* rate.
b. He tried **for** many years to become a lawyer.
c. They used their house **for** collateral.

2. **for** - in place of something or someone

a. "I'll do* it **for** you," offered her friend.
b. It will do* **for** now until the car is fixed.
c. She did the assignment **for** her brother.

3 **for** - in favor of something or someone

a. The citizens were **for** the idea.
b. "I'm **for** the president," shouted a man in the aisle*.
c. The citizens' group is **for** building a new dam*.

4 **fore** - used by a golfer as a warning

a. On the crowded course* the golfer yelled, "**Fore**!"
b. "Don't forget to yell, **fore**, before you hit the ball," warned the golf instructor.
c. "I didn't hear him yell **fore**!" griped the man.

5 **fore** - in front of; very important

a. Trade barriers will be* in the **fore** again this year.
b. This problem will come to the **fore** if it isn't solved now.
c. The speaker came to the **fore** to air* her opinion.

6 **four** - the number four; 4

a. My friend has **four** sisters.
b. **Four** children caught the flu* at the fair*.
c. The meeting starts at **four** o'clock.

***Previously Used Words**

birth
do
aisle
dam
course
be
air
flu
fair

Practice Exercises on next page.

for / fore / four

PRACTICE EXERCISES

✎ ***Write the correct word in the blank space. (Answers at bottom.)***

1. Nobody was ________________ raising taxes.
2. Again and again the same problem came to the ________________.
3. Only ________________ people showed up at the meeting.
4. She'll do the job ________________ him.
5. They got the award ________________ saving the man from drowning.

✎ ***Write your own sentences.***

1. ____
2. ____
3. ____
4. ____
5. ____
6. ____

Answers: 1. for 2. fore 3. four 4. for 5. for

gnu / knew / new

Study these words to learn their differences.

1 **gnu** - a large African antelope

a. In the distance we saw a herd of **gnu**.
b. The zoo has only one **gnu**.
c. Most people don't know what a **gnu** looks like.

Note: The plural of *gnu* can be *gnu* or *gnus*.

2 **knew** - past tense of know; to have understood

a. The mother **knew** her son was lying when he wouldn't look at her.
b. I **knew** then that she wouldn't come.
c. When I saw the test I **knew** I couldn't pass it.

3 **new** - very recent; modern; not old

a. My sister bought a **new** car.
b. He is one of the **new** employees.
c. Her ideas are **new** and refreshing.

Note: Also, *brand new* means extremely new. Example: They just brought their *brand new* baby home from the hospital.

PRACTICE EXERCISES

Write the correct word in the blank space. (Answers at bottom.)

1. Have you ever seen a ________________?
2. I ________________ he couldn't do it.
3. He can't afford to buy a ________________ car.
4. They ________________ each other a long time ago.
5. She wants a ________________ computer.

Write your own sentences.

1. ____
2. ____
3. ____

Answers: 1. gnu 2. knew 3. new 4. knew 5. new

groan / grown

Study these words to learn their differences.

*Previously Used Words
flee
damn

1 **groan** - to utter a moan to show pain, grief, disappointment, or annoyance

a. The injured man let out a **groan** as he tried to flee*.
b. His pun made everyone **groan**.
c. The student started to **groan** when he read his final grade.

2 **grown** - past tense of grow; to become mature; adult

a. "I have **grown** tired of your damn* complaining," stated his angry wife.
b. All of her children are **grown** and married.
c. She is a **grown** woman and can make her own decisions.

Note: The word *grown-up* is also used to mean adult. Example: He doesn't act like a *grown-up*.

PRACTICE EXERCISES

Write the correct word in the blank space. (Answers at bottom.)

1. The dog started to ________________.
2. All the trees have ________________ a foot in height.
3. His mother was surprised to see how much he had ________________.
4. When the irate shopper complained the clerk began to ________________.
5. Many citizens have ________________ weary of voting.

Write your own sentences.

1. ____
2. ____

Answers: 1. groan 2. grown 3. grown 4. groan 5. grown

hail / hale

Study these words to learn their differences.

*Previously Used Words
break
flour
cereal
for

1 **hail** - frozen rain

a. We were caught in a **hail** storm.
b. They hoped the **hail** wouldn't break* the windows.
c. The **hail** ruined all the flour* and cereal*.

2 **hail** - to greet enthusiastically

a. "**Hail** to the queen," cried the people.
b. His girlfriend began to **hail** him as he stepped off the train.
c. As the lovers drew closer they began to **hail** each other.

3 **hail** - to call or attract attention

a. It is difficult to **hail** a taxi in New York City.
b. The woman tried to **hail** a porter in the crowded terminal.
c. He tried desperately to **hail** a driver in the night.

4 **hale** - free from defect or disease; sound; healthy; vigorous

a. For* her age she is really **hale** and hearty.
b. If you take vitamins you'll be **hale** all your life.
c. "**Hale** means the same as healthy," explained the teacher.

5 **hale** - to haul; to carry

a. The old man tried to **hale** the load on his back.
b. If you overload a camel it will simply refuse to **hale** the burden.
c. The old bus used to **hale** the students to school.

Note: Nowadays most people use the word *haul* instead of *hale*.

Practice Exercises on next page.

hail / hale

PRACTICE EXERCISES

Write the correct word in the blank space. (Answers at bottom.)

1. All of the sudden ______________ started to fall.
2. The crowd began to ______________ their hero.
3. It was difficult for me to ______________ the load of wood.
4. The desperate boy tried to ______________ a passing car.
5. She looked ______________ for her age.

Write your own sentences.

1. ____
2. ____
3. ____
4. ____
5. ____

Answers: 1. hail 2. hail 3. hale 4. hail 5. hale

hair / hare

Study these words to learn their differences.

*Previously Used Words
ferry
flower

1 **hair** - the hairy covering of man or animal

a. A bald person has no **hair** on his head.
b. The captain of the ferry* had long blond **hair**.
c. The collie's **hair** was soft and clean.

2 **hare** - a furry animal that looks like a rabbit

a. A famous children's story is called *The Tortoise and the Hare*.
b. His dog chased the **hare** into the flower* garden.
c. The hunter caught a **hare** in his trap.

Note: The plural of *hare* can be *hare* or *hares*.

PRACTICE EXERCISES

Write the correct word in the blank space. (Answers at bottom.)

1. Her black __________________ glistened in the moonlight.
2. The __________________ ran through the field of corn.
3. Jimmy's pet __________________ escaped from its pen.
4. The barber cut my __________________ too short.
5. I like her new __________________ style.

Write your own sentences.

1. ____
2. ____

Answers: 1. hair 2. hare 3. hare 4. hair 5. hair

hall / haul

Study these words to learn their differences.

*Previously Used Words
fir
by
aisle
bin
ferry

1 **hall** - an entrance room or passageway in a house or building

a. Many students were talking in the **hall**.
b. The walls in the **hall** were made of fir*.
c. They walked by* each other in the **hall** but said nothing.

Note: *Hall* is often referred to as *hallway*.

2 **hall** - a very large room; an auditorium

a. Carnegie **Hall** is located in New York City.
b. The beer **hall** was filled to capacity.
c. There was standing room only in the center aisle* of the music **hall**.

3 **haul** - to carry a load

a. The big truck could **haul** a heavy load.
b. A tanker can **haul** large amounts of oil.
c. The old man was too weak to **haul** the heavy trash bin*.

4 **haul** - the distance that a load is carried; the distance of a trip

a. It's a long **haul** from L.A. to Seattle by ferry*.
b. Some passengers got weary from the long **haul** on the plane.
c. He liked to drive the short **haul** from Phoenix to San Diego.

PRACTICE EXERCISES

Write the correct word in the blank space. (Answers at bottom.)

1. The __________________ in their house is long and dark.
2. Ron's pick-up truck could __________________ a lot of wood.
3. They had the rock concert in the city __________________.
4. It was a long __________________ from Texas to Alaska.
5. The school __________________ was packed with late students.

Write your own sentences.

1. ____
2. ____
3. ____
4. ____

Answers: 1. hall 2. haul 3. hall 4. haul 5. hall

hangar / hanger

Study these words to learn their differences.

1 **hangar** - an enclosed area for repairing or parking aircraft

a. The airplane is in the **hangar** for* repairs.
b. Rental space in a **hangar** is expensive.
c. The plane engine blew* dust all over the **hangar**.

2 **hanger** - something used to hang clothes on

a. There's a **hanger** in the hall* closet.
b. Is there a **hanger** for my pants?
c. The **hanger** comes with the suit.

***Previously Used Words**

for
blew
hall

PRACTICE EXERCISES

Write the correct word in the blank space. (Answers at bottom.)

1. The pilot parked his airplane in the ________________.
2. Can I borrow a coat ________________?
3. She smacked the cat with a wire ________________.
4. The ________________ was in the middle of the airport.
5. Every ________________ in the closet was made of cedar.

Write your own sentences.

1. ____
2. ____

Answers: 1. hangar 2. hanger 3. hanger 4. hangar 5. hanger

heal / heel

Study these words to learn their differences.

***Previously Used Words**

for
deer
be

1 **heal** – to make better; to get well

a. It takes a long time for* a broken bone to **heal**.
b. The injury did not **heal** well.
c. The emotional wounds from his insult took a long time to **heal**.

2 **heel** – the back part of a foot

a. I bruised my **heel** playing football.
b. She had a pain in her left **heel**.
c. The doctor had to operate on the player's **heel**.

3 **heel** – the back portion of a shoe

a. The **heel** of my shoe fell off when I was chasing the deer*.
b. I always wear down the **heel** of my right shoe.
c. "Can you repair this **heel**?" asked the woman to the cobbler.

4 **heel** – a contemptible individual

a. He's a real **heel**.
b. You have to be* a **heel** to steal from your friends.
c. The hero in the movie turned out to be* a **heel**.

PRACTICE EXERCISES

Write the correct word in the blank space. (Answers at bottom.)

1. Jeff is nothing but a ________________.
2. The man said he could ________________ any sick person.
3. My brother cut his ________________ on a piece of glass.
4. The ________________ on my left shoe was put on crooked.
5. Not even the best doctors could ________________ the dying man.

Write your own sentences.

1. ____
2. ____
3. ____
4. ____

Answers: 1. heel 2. heal 3. heel 4. heel 5. heal

hear / here

Study these words to learn their differences.

***Previously Used Words**
gnu
born
eight
be
hail

1 **hear** - to listen; to perceive by ear

a. The deaf man couldn't **hear** what the little girl said.
b. It was hard to **hear** the speaker.
c. Every day you can **hear** the chimes of Big Ben in London.

Note: An easy way to remember this word is that the word *ear* is within the word *hear*.

2 **here** - this place

a. That gnu* was born* **here** eight* years ago.
b. They'll be* **here** in a few minutes.
c. I'm glad we got **here** before it started to hail*.

3 **here** - used when answering roll call

a. "Please say **here** when your name is called," said the instructor.
b. The pupil forgot to answer **here** and was marked absent.
c. In some schools children must stand and say **here** when roll is taken.

PRACTICE EXERCISES

Write the correct word in the blank space. (Answers at bottom.)

1. It was difficult to ________________ over all the noise.
2. Let's meet ________________ at six o'clock.
3. Did you ________________ what the instructor said?
4. Please set the boxes down ________________.
5. He didn't ________________ a word I said

Write your own sentences.

1. ____
2. ____
3. ____

Answers: 1. hear 2. here 3. hear 4. here 5. hear

heard / herd

Study these words to learn their differences.

1 **heard** - past tense of hear; to have listened or perceived something by ear

a. I haven't **heard** the stock market report yet.
b. **Heard** any good jokes lately?
c. Apparently, Tom hasn't **heard** the bad news.

2 **herd** - a group of the same kind of animals

a. The cowboys drove the **herd** of cattle to the train station.
b. All the calves were separated from the **herd**.
c. Poachers hunted the **herd** of wild elephants at night.

Note: Not all animal groups are called a *herd*. Sometimes they are different according to what kind of animal it is. Elephants, cattle, and horses are usually referred to in a group as a *herd*. Some examples of other groups of animals are: a *band* of gorillas; a *brace* of ducks; a *crash* of rhinoceri; a *murder* of crows; a *pride* of lions; a *school* of fish, etc.

PRACTICE EXERCISES

Write the correct word in the blank space. (Answers at bottom.)

1. Have you ever seen a ________________ of wild horses?
2. I haven't ________________ from her in six months.
3. The ________________ of cattle started to stampede.
4. She ________________ the news on the radio.
5. We ________________ the noise from our neighbor's party.

Write your own sentences.

1. ____
2. ____

Answers: 1. herd 2. heard 3. herd 4. heard 5. heard

hi / high

Study these words to learn their differences.

*Previously Used Words
flew
air
grown

1 **hi** - used as a greeting; hello

a. "**Hi**! How are you?" called the pretty coed.
b. She is still mad and wouldn't even say **hi**.
c. I always say **hi** to our neighbor.

2 **high** - very tall

a. Nepal has many **high** mountains.
b. He built his house **high** on the hill.
c. The rocket flew* **high** into the air*.

Note: When talking about a person's height we do not say he is very ***high***. Instead, we say he is very ***tall***.

3 **high** - under the influence of drugs or alcohol

a. He got **high** after smoking marijuana.
b. The grown* man was so **high** he couldn't walk.
c. In the 60s many people got **high**.

4 **high** - having to do with the weather and amount of degrees in temperature; pressure in the atmosphere

a. The **high** for today was 32 degrees.
b. The temperature didn't go as **high** as I thought it would.
c. A **high** pressure system formed over the mountains.

Practice Exercises on next page.

hi / high

PRACTICE EXERCISES

✎ ***Write the correct word in the blank space. (Answers at bottom.)***

1. The stranger waved and shouted, "________________."
2. The new building wasn't very ________________.
3. How ________________ did the temperature get today?
4. Many religions don't like people to get ________________.
5. Some people say hello instead of ________________.

✎ ***Write your own sentences.***

1. ____
2. ____
3. ____
4. ____

Answers: 1. hi 2. high 3. high 4. high 5. hi

him / hymn

Study these words to learn their differences.

***Previously Used Words**
hear
hangar

1 **him** - objective case of he

a. She couldn't hear* **him** because it was too noisy.
b. I saw **him** yesterday in the hangar*.
c. That book belongs to **him**.

2 **hymn** - a song of praise or joy

a. The church choir sang only one **hymn**.
b. All the people joined in singing the **hymn**.
c. My favorite **hymn** is "Amazing Grace."

PRACTICE EXERCISES

✎ *Write the correct word in the blank space. (Answers at bottom.)*

1. "I am sure I saw ________________," said the witness.
2. They pointed at ________________ and started to laugh.
3. The woman sang our favorite ________________.
4. She doesn't like ________________ anymore.
5. Everyone sang the ________________ off key.

✎ *Write your own sentences.*

1. ____
2. ____

Answers: 1. him 2. him 3. hymn 4. him 5. hymn

hoarse / horse

Study these words to learn their differences.

1 **hoarse** – rough in sound

a. His voice was **hoarse** from shouting during the game.
b. My voice is **hoarse** because I have the flu*.
c. She has a sore throat and her voice is **hoarse**.

2 **horse** – a large animal used for work or riding

a. The children came here* to see the **horse**.
b. His **horse** could haul* the bag of flour* very easily.
c. A **horse** is a cowboy's best friend.

***Previously Used Words**

flu
here
haul
flour

PRACTICE EXERCISES

Write the correct word in the blank space. (Answers at bottom.)

1. His voice was ________________ because he smoked too much.
2. The ________________ was beautiful when it ran in the race.
3. A ________________ doesn't pollute the way a car does.
4. His singing voice sounded ________________ to me.
5. It costs a lot of money to own a ________________.

Write your own sentences.

1. ____
2. ____

Answers: 1. hoarse 2. horse 3. horse 4. hoarse 5. horse

hole / whole

Study these words to learn their differences.

*Previously Used Words
fur
flower
bury
due
ate
berry
hall

1 **hole** - an opening in or through something

a. There's a **hole** in her fur* coat.
b. My gas tank has a **hole** in it.
c. I patched the **hole** in my bicycle inner tube.

2 **hole** - an area dug out of the ground

a. He dug a **hole** and planted the flower*.
b. The soldier dug a **hole** and climbed inside.
c. We decided to dig a **hole** and bury* the dead cat.

3 **whole** - the complete amount

a. The **whole** amount is due* next month.
b. Her child ate* the **whole** berry* pie.
c. I was late getting to the hall* so I couldn't see the **whole** play.

PRACTICE EXERCISES

Write the correct word in the blank space. (Answers at bottom.)

1. There was a ________________ in my new pants.
2. The girls dug a ________________ to plant the bush.
3. The executives sold the ________________ company.
4. My mother repaired the ________________ in the wall.
5. The ________________ school turned out for the game.

Write your own sentences.

1. ____
2. ____
3. ____

Answers: 1. hole 2. hole 3. whole 4. hole 5. whole

hostile / hostel

Study these words to learn their differences.

***Previously Used Words**
be
high
break

1 **hostile** - unfriendly; antagonistic

a. The man knew the student would be* **hostile**.
b. The **hostile** woman attacked the security guard.
c. He was **hostile** to everyone because he was high*.

Note: There are two ways of pronouncing this word. Check your dictionary for details.

2 **hostel** - a lodging house usually for young travelers; inn

a. The youth **hostel** is high* in the mountains.
b. He stayed at the **hostel** because it was inexpensive.
c. They stopped at the **hostel** to take a break*.

PRACTICE EXERCISES

Write the correct word in the blank space. (Answers at bottom.)

1. The __________ man repeatedly yelled at the police.
2. This city's __________ is very clean.
3. Susan was sad because she lost her ring in the __________.
4. It's difficult to talk to a __________ person.
5. Let's spend the night at the __________.

Write your own sentences.

1. ______________________________
2. ______________________________

Answers: 1. hostile 2. hostel 3. hostel 4. hostile 5. hostel

hour / our

Study these words to learn their differences.

***Previously Used Words**
- ball
- capitol
- groan
- horse
- feet

1 **hour** - equal to 60 minutes

a. I study English for one **hour** everyday.
b. He was an **hour** late to the ball*.
c. The train will arrive in an **hour**.

2 **our** - ourselves; us

a. **Our** house is next to the capitol*.
b. We heard **our** friend groan* as the horse* stepped on both of his feet*.
c. He is **our** science teacher.

PRACTICE EXERCISES

Write the correct word in the blank space. (Answers at bottom.)

1. We have to wait for an ________________.
2. The airline company lost all of ________________ baggage.
3. These are not ________________ tickets.
4. It takes only an ________________ by train.
5. That is ________________ dog.

Write your own sentences.

1. ____
2. ____

Answers: 1. hour 2. our 3. our 4. hour 5. our

idle / idol / idyll

Study these words to learn their differences.

*Previously Used Words
flair
by
heel
our
altar
be
bore
do

1 **idle** - worthless; without basis

a. That woman has a flair* for **idle** chatter.
b. All he did was make **idle** threats.
c. The **idle** student sat by* the window staring outside.

2 **idle** - not scheduled to play or compete

a. The player will be **idle** until his injured heel* is better.
b. Our* team is **idle** every other Wednesday.
c. Last week the Little League team was **idle**.

3 **idle** - to run disconnected, without useful power

a. Car engines have a low **idle** speed.
b. He put the machine in neutral and let the engine **idle**.
c. The boat engine would not **idle** properly.

4 **idol** - a symbol of worship

a. Some religions believe in **idol** worship.
b. The **idol** was placed in the middle of the altar*.
c. The **idol** was made of stone.

5 **idol** - a screen star who is very popular

a. She may be* a Hollywood **idol**, but I think she is a real bore*.
b. Clark Gable was a famous **idol**.
c. My daughter doesn't have a favorite movie **idol**.

6 **idyll** - a simple work of prose or poetry relating to a peaceful feeling

a. The poem was an **idyll** of country life.
b. I thought the **idyll** was not so interesting.
c. She had to do* a report on an **idyll** by* Robert Browning.

Note: This word can also be spelled *idyl*, with the same pronunciation and meaning.

Practice Exercises on next page

idle / idol / idyll

PRACTICE EXERCISES

✎ *Write the correct word in the blank space. (Answers at bottom.)*

1. The soccer team was ________________ today.
2. Karen adjusted the ________________ on the engine.
3. Most people have a favorite movie ________________.
4. Her poem won a prize for showing the ________________ countryside.
5. They didn't take the ________________ threat seriously.

✎ *Write your own sentences.*

1. ____
2. ____
3. ____
4. ____
5. ____
6. ____

Answers: 1. idle 2. idle 3. idol 4. idyll 5. idle

in / inn

Study these words to learn their differences.

1 **in** - within a boundary or limit

a. My father was born **in** Ohio.
b. The prisoner is **in** his cell*.
c. The whole* class is **in** the recital hall*.

2 **in** - inside

a. The child **in** the car began to bawl*.
b. He put the cake **in** the box.
c. The baker wrapped the loaf of bread* **in** paper.

3 **inn** - a place for travelers to eat and sleep

a. We stayed overnight at the **inn**.
b. Another word for **inn** is hostel.*
c. The **inn** near here* has a cozy atmosphere.

4 **inn** - tavern

a. The **inn** was full of customers drinking beer because it was happy hour*.
b. She went with him* to the **inn** after the movie.
c. The old **inn** finally went out of business.

***Previously Used Words**

cell
whole
hall
bawl
bread
hostel
here
hour
him

PRACTICE EXERCISES

Write the correct word in the blank space. (Answers at bottom.)

1. She lives ________________ the city.
2. The ________________ was cheap and had good food.
3. The car is ________________ the garage.
4. We stopped at the ________________ for a beer.
5. They bought the ________________ as an investment.

Write your own sentences.

1. ____
2. ____
3. ____
4. ____

Answers: 1. in 2. inn 3. in 4. inn 5. inn

knight / night

Study these words to learn their differences.

1 **knight** – a man honored by a king or queen for exceptional service

- a. The official title of a **knight** is *Sir*.
- b. The **knight** held out his hand to the lady.
- c. A famous **knight** in* British folklore is Sir Lancelot.

2 **night** – the time from dusk to dawn; no sunlight; dark

- a. Last **night** I worked an hour* overtime in* the hangar*.
- b. The whole* **night** was wet and rainy.
- c. The television ad* was only shown at **night**.

***Previously Used Words**

in
hour
hangar
whole
ad

PRACTICE EXERCISES

Write the correct word in the blank space. (Answers at bottom.)

1. The ________________ in the movie was tall and handsome.
2. Every ________________ her husband comes home late.
3. The full moon lit up the ________________ sky.
4. It is dangerous to walk at ________________ in big cities.
5. The ________________ killed the dragon with his sword.

Write your own sentences.

1. ____
2. ____

Answers: 1. knight 2. night 3. night 4. night 5. knight

knot / not

Study these words to learn their differences.

1 **knot** - the tied up portion of string, rope, ribbon, etc., that forms a lump or knob

a. The fisherman tied the rope into a **knot**.
b. Keep the **knot** just below your fingers.
c. A trucker's **knot** is very convenient when you haul* things.

2 **not** - something or someone in the negative; no

a. I do **not** like him*.
b. She said she does **not** want to change her hair*style.
c. He is **not** for* the idea.

***Previously Used Words**

haul
him
hair
for

PRACTICE EXERCISES

Write the correct word in the blank space. (Answers at bottom.)

1. It is ________________ a good idea.
2. He did ________________ have the right answer.
3. The ________________ came loose, so the rope fell off the truck.
4. I'm ________________ sure where she lives.
5. Make sure you tie the ________________ very tight.

Write your own sentences.

1. ____
2. ____

Answers: 1. not 2. not 3. knot 4. not 5. knot

know / no

Study these words to learn their differences.

1 **know** - to perceive correctly; to understand
- a. Do* you **know** what the capital* of the United States is?
- b. She doesn't **know** where to buy* any good dessert*.
- c. I don't **know** how to light this flare*.

2 **no** - denial; refusal; negative; opposite of yes
- a. She said "**no**" when I asked her to marry me.
- b. Some parents automatically say **no** to everything their children ask.
- c. "**No**, I think you made an error when you tried to add* the numbers," said the customer.

***Previously Used Words**

do
capital
buy
dessert
flare
add

PRACTICE EXERCISES

✎ ***Write the correct word in the blank space. (Answers at bottom.)***

1. "I ________________ how to make pizza," said Ken.
2. The new actor doesn't ________________ his part yet.
3. He said ________________ to my idea.
4. Do you ________________ who she is?
5. ________________, you can't come with me.

✎ ***Write your own sentences.***

1. ____
2. ____

Answers: 1. know 2. know 3. no 4. know 5. No

lie / lye

Study these words to learn their differences.

1 **lie** - to be in, or put into, a horizontal position

a. My dog likes to **lie** in* front of the fireplace.
b. The injured man was told to **lie** down next to the aisle*.
c. After the defeat our* whole* team chose to **lie** on the field for nearly an hour*.

2 **lie** - not the truth; not honest; dishonest

a. Sometimes salespeople will **lie** to you.
b. A **lie** will usually catch up to you.
c. She scolded her son because he told a **lie**.

Note: A *white lie* is not a serious lie and is sometimes called a *fib*. Example: Barbara told a *white lie* when she told her mother that she made the cake from scratch.

3 **lye** - an alkaline solution of varying strength and degree

a. **Lye** is used to make soap.
b. The baby was allergic to the **lye** in* the shampoo.
c. Nondiluted **lye** must be handled very carefully.

***Previously Used Words**

in
aisle
our
whole
hour

PRACTICE EXERCISES

Write the correct word in the blank space. (Answers at bottom.)

1. The senator told the committee one ________________ after another.
2. "Don't ________________ to me," demanded her angry father.
3. The ________________ in soap is what burns your eyes.
4. I want to ________________ down for awhile.
5. Industrial soap has a large amount of ________________ in it.

Write your own sentences.

1. ____
2. ____
3. ____

Answers: 1. lie 2. lie 3. lye 4. lie 5. lye

loan / lone

Study these words to learn their differences.

*Previously Used Words
bread
new
not

1 **loan** - something given for temporary use

a. Can you **loan** me some bread?*
b. I'm going to take out a bank **loan** for a new* house.
c. It's not* a good idea to **loan** money to strangers.

2 **lone** - by one's self; the only one; alone

a. We could hear the **lone** wolf cry at night.
b. I always enjoyed watching the **Lone** Ranger on television.
c. He was the **lone** foreigner at the party.

PRACTICE EXERCISES

✎ *Write the correct word in the blank space. (Answers at bottom.)*

1. The bank didn't approve my ________________.
2. At night the ________________ person on the street walked quickly.
3. Can you ________________ me $50?
4. Dr. Howard was the ________________ professor at the meeting.
5. Make sure you pay back the ________________.

✎ *Write your own sentences.*

1. ____
2. ____

Answers: 1. loan 2. lone 3. loan 4. lone 5. loan

made / maid

Study these words to learn their differences.

1 **made** – past tense of make; to have put together or produced something

a. I **made** a coffee table last weekend.
b. She **made** a part that fit exactly into the computer.
c. The whole* class **made** something for our* party.

2 **made** – to have done something; to have caused something to happen

a. He said something that **made** the censor* mad.
b. The manager **made** the right decision.
c. That lady **made** a lot of money selling new* clothes.

3 **maid** – a female servant

a. Many rich people have a **maid** and a butler.
b. His **maid** did all the cooking and house cleaning.
c. Our* **maid** has worked here* for* eight* years.

***Previously Used Words**

whole
our
censor
new
here
for
eight

PRACTICE EXERCISES

Write the correct word in the blank space. (Answers at bottom.)

1. I ____________________ coffee for everybody.
2. His uncle gave the ____________________ a two-week vacation.
3. She ____________________ a fortune selling houses.
4. Their ____________________ was a very hard worker.
5. "I ____________________ my bed," said the boy to his mother.

Write your own sentences.

1. ____
2. ____
3. ____

Answers: 1. made 2. maid 3. made 4. maid 5. made

mail / male

Study these words to learn their differences.

*Previously Used Words
bore
ad
in
lone

1 **mail** – letters, postcards, packages and other things sent through a postal service system

a. Reading junk **mail** is a bore*.
b. I usually get **mail** every day.
c. Bob received the supermarket ad* in* the **mail**.

2 **mail** – to send letters, postcards, and other things through a postal service

a. "Would you **mail** this, please?" asked my mother.
b. I forgot to **mail** all the postcards.
c. She will **mail** the package before she goes home.

3 **male** – a boy or man; not female

a. Japan is a **male** dominated society.
b. The club only allowed **male** members.
c. There was only a lone* **male** puppy in* the litter.

PRACTICE EXERCISES

Write the correct word in the blank space. (Answers at bottom.)

1. Don't forget to ________________ the letter.
2. Did the ________________ come yet?
3. She didn't appreciate his ________________ point of view.
4. The ________________ was late today.
5. Many young boys do not have good ________________ role models to follow.

Write your own sentences.

1. ____
2. ____
3. ____

Answers: 1. mail 2. mail 3. male 4. mail 5. male

marry / merry

Study these words to learn their differences.

*Previously Used Words
hale
inn
in

1 **marry** - to become husband and wife

a. He wants to **marry** her but he's afraid to ask.
b. Many women don't want to **marry** until they get older.
c. They intend to **marry** each other next year.

2 **merry** - happy; delightful; not sad

a. The **merry** old couple seemed hale* and hearty even after 60 years of marriage.
b. Everybody at the inn* was in* a **merry** mood.
c. She was always shy and never seemed **merry**.

Note: *Mary* is also the name for a woman with the same pronunciation but different spelling.

PRACTICE EXERCISES

Write the correct word in the blank space. (Answers at bottom.)

1. The ________________ group of people began to sing.
2. She decided not to ________________ him.
3. It is a crazy idea to ________________ for money.
4. Our party had a ________________ atmosphere.
5. It's better to be ________________ than depressed.

Write your own sentences.

1. ____
2. ____

Answers: 1. merry 2. marry 3. marry 4. merry 5. merry

meat / meet / mete

Study these words to learn their differences.

*Previously Used Words
ate
night
maid
I'll
hostel
heard
here
by
capitol
hail
in

1 **meat** - flesh to be eaten

a. Vegetarians don't eat **meat**.
b. His dog ate* **meat** every night*.
c. The maid* served everyone **meat** and potatoes.

2 **meet** - to come or get together at some set time or place

a. I'll* **meet** you at six o'clock next to the hostel*.
b. I heard* they were going to **meet** here.*
c. Let's **meet** at the bus station by* the capitol* building.

3 **meet** - a get together for sports competition

a. There is a track **meet** this Saturday.
b. The **meet** was postponed because of sleet and hail*.
c. Many sports stars competed in* the **meet**.

4 **mete** - to give out by measure

a. The teacher threatened to **mete** out strict punishment.
b. Some leaders **mete** out harsh reprimands to their aides.
c. I am sure the boss will **mete** out a heavy warning to him.

Note: The word *out* is usually used after *mete*.

PRACTICE EXERCISES

Write the correct word in the blank space. (Answers at bottom.)

1. My sister doesn't eat ________________.
2. Let's ________________ again next summer.
3. The star runner failed to show up for the track ________________.
4. Red wine goes well with red ________________.
5. The sergeant began to ________________ out punishment to the troops.

Write your own sentences.

1. ____
2. ____
3. ____
4. ____

Answers: 1. meat 2. meet 3. meet 4. meat 5. mete.

morning / mourning

Study these words to learn their differences.

***Previously Used Words**
for
hair
whole
heard

1 **morning** – from midnight to noon; a.m.

a. She usually gets up late every **morning**.
b. It's always hard for* me to wake up on Monday **morning**.
c. Every **morning** my hair* is difficult to comb.

2 **mourning** – to express grief or sorrow over a death

a. The whole* nation is **mourning** the loss of its leader.
b. **Mourning** could be heard* all over the city after the attack.
c. The family entered a state of **mourning** after her death.

PRACTICE EXERCISES

Write the correct word in the blank space. (Answers at bottom.)

1. After the queen's death everyone was ________________.
2. He always brushes his teeth in the ________________.
3. I eat breakfast every ________________.
4. Yesterday ________________ I got up late.
5. The ________________ lasted for one week.

Write your own sentences.

1. ____
2. ____

Answers: 1. mourning 2. morning 3. morning 4. morning 5. mourning

one / won

Study these words to learn their differences.

*Previously Used Words
meet
by
hymn
hole
bury
our
lone
knight

1 **one** – the number one; 1

a. My son is **one** year old.
b. The sports meet* starts at **one** o'clock.
c. Her address is, **One** Taylor Street, Ogden, Utah.

2 **one** – a single unit, person, place, or thing

a. **One** of my friends dropped by* my house yesterday.
b. Only **one** person disagreed with singing the hymn*.
c. They dug **one** big hole* to bury* all the stolen money.

3 **won** – past and past participle of win; to have been victorious; succeeded; opposite of lost

a. Our* team **won** the championship.
b. The basketball team finally **won** a game.
c. The lone* knight* never **won** a tournament.

PRACTICE EXERCISES.

Write the correct word in the blank space. (Answers at bottom.)

1. There was only ________________ person in the room.
2. We ________________ the game in overtime.
3. You must dial zero zero ________________ when making an overseas call.
4. I have only ________________ question.
5. Their team has never ________________ a game in this stadium.

Write your own sentences.

1. ____
2. ____
3. ____

Answers: 1. one 2. won 3. one 4. one 5. won

pail / pale

Study these words to learn their differences.

***Previously Used Words**

haul
in
groan
born

1 **pail** - a bucket

a. The **pail** had rusted completely through.
b. She will haul* the water in* the **pail**.
c. Linda began to groan*, "I knew this store wouldn't have the right size **pail**."

2 **pale** - lacking color; pallid

a. Upon receiving the bad news his face turned **pale**.
b. When it was born*, the baby looked weak and **pale**.
c. Her **pale** face reflected against the moonlight.

PRACTICE EXERCISES

Write the correct word in the blank space. (Answers at bottom.)

1. The ________________ was old and rusty.
2. He turned as ________________ as a ghost.
3. The farmer put the feed in a ________________.
4. Doug's face went ________________ when he saw the blood.
5. She was ________________ from lack of sleep.

Write your own sentences.

1. ____
2. ____

Answers: 1. pail 2. pale 3. pail 4. pale 5. pale

pain / pane

Study these words to learn their differences.

***Previously Used Words**

heel
bear
not
break

1 **pain** – to suffer physical or mental distress; hurt

a. Sometimes I have a terrible back **pain**.
b. The sprinter had **pain** from his hip to his heel*.
c. The **pain** of knowing her father was an alcoholic was a heavy burden to bear*.

2 **pane** – a sheet of glass

a. He tried not* to break* the **pane** of glass.
b. The glass **pane** was composed of many different colors.
c. The **pane** didn't fit the window frame.

PRACTICE EXERCISES

Write the correct word in the blank space. (Answers at bottom.)

1. The __________________ from a broken heart can hurt more than a real wound.
2. His toothache caused him a lot of __________________.
3. The construction worker dropped the __________________ of glass.
4. Mr. Smith replaced the broken __________________ in his greenhouse.
5. The __________________ of his wife's death was too difficult for him to handle.

Write your own sentences.

1. ____
2. ____

Answers: 1. pain 2. pain 3. pane 4. pane 5. pain

pair / pare / pear

Study these words to learn their differences.

*Previously Used Words
new
for
here
won
one
in
our
loan

1 **pair** - two things that are to be used together

a. Yesterday I bought a new* **pair** of shoes.
b. I gave her a **pair** of gloves for* her birthday.
c. The socks weren't of the same **pair**.

2 **pair** - a couple

a. They are a perfect **pair**.
b. The same **pair** of pigeons nest here* every year.
c. That **pair** of dancers won* first prize.

3 **pare** - to trim or cut off; to peal

a. The company is going to **pare** some of its older employees.
b. The government must **pare** down the budget.
c. His grandmother used to **pare** apples during the summer.

4 **pear** - a sweet fruit that grows on trees

a. We have one* **pear** tree in* our* garden.
b. He took out a bank loan* to start a **pear** farm.
c. A Japanese **pear** is different from an American **pear**.

PRACTICE EXERCISES

Write the correct word in the blank space. (Answers at bottom.)

1. The ________________ of bookends didn't match.
2. They decided to ________________ down their entertainment expenses.
3. I picked a ________________ from the tree and ate it.
4. Joan and Frank make a really nice ________________.
5. The new ________________ of scissors were very sharp.

Write your own sentences.

1. ____
2. ____
3. ____
4. ____

Answers: **1. pair 2. pare 3. pear 4. pair 5. pair**

peace / piece

Study these words to learn their differences.

***Previously Used Words**
be
pane

1 **peace** – friendship; harmony; not fighting; opposite of war

a. World **peace** should be* the common goal of all governments.
b. Which is more profitable, war or **peace**?
c. After talking with his son the father was at **peace** with himself.

2 **piece** – a portion; part of the whole

a. "May I have another **piece** of cake?" asked the child.
b. A **piece** of the broken pane* shattered on the ground.
c. The greedy salesman wanted a **piece** of all the action.

PRACTICE EXERCISES

Write the correct word in the blank space. (Answers at bottom.)

1. "Is world ________________ really possible?" asked the philosopher.
2. They were missing one ________________ from the jigsaw puzzle.
3. The ________________ of chalk fell on the floor.
4. "________________ does not come cheaply," warned the speaker.
5. He ate every ________________ of cake on the plate.

Write your own sentences.

1. ____
2. ____

Answers: 1. peace 2. piece 3. piece 4. Peace 5. piece

peak / peek / pique

Study these words to learn their differences.

*Previously Used Words
idol
made
not
night
morning
hostile

1 **peak** – at the top; the highest point

a. The idol* is at the **peak** of her career.
b. Only a handful of people have ever made* it to the **peak** of Mt. Everest.
c. The team tried not* to **peak** too soon.

2 **peek** – a quick look; a glance

a. "Don't **peek**!" squealed the boy.
b. Last night* he snuck a **peek** at the attractive girl.
c. The dishonest student tried to **peek** at his neighbor's test.

3 **pique** – to arouse anger; to irritate

a. Every morning* Mr. Allen was careful not to **pique** his wife.
b. The speaker tried not* to **pique** the hostile* audience.
c. It's dangerous to **pique** someone bigger than you.

PRACTICE EXERCISES

Write the correct word in the blank space. (Answers at bottom.)

1. His constant chattering started to ________________ the customer.
2. Jerry couldn't help taking a ________________ at the present.
3. They reached the ________________ in record time.
4. "Promise not to ________________," said the new bride.
5. Mrs. Johnson is at the ________________ of her career.

Write your own sentences.

1. ____
2. ____
3. ____

Answers: **1. pique 2. peek 3. peak 4. peek 5. peak**

plain / plane

*Previously Used Words
knew
in
flew
high

Study these words to learn their differences.

1 **plain** - lacking ornaments; undecorated

a. I like to eat **plain** donuts.
b. She was a very **plain** looking girl.
c. His life was **plain** and uninteresting.

2 **plane** - a tool used for smoothing or shaving wood

a. The apprentice carpenter knew* how to use a **plane**.
b. The blade on the **plane** was dull.
c. In* America you push a **plane**, but in* Japan you pull it.

3 **plane** - an airplane

a. Terrorists hijacked the **plane**.
b. The **plane** flew* high* over the clouds.
c. Her **plane** took off from San Francisco Airport.

PRACTICE EXERCISES

✎ *Write the correct word in the blank space. (Answers at bottom.)*

1. All the ________________ cakes were on sale.
2. The woodworker cut her finger with the ________________.
3. The ________________ took off on time.
4. Her ________________ wedding band was very expensive.
5. After a while the ________________ came into sight.

✎ *Write your own sentences.*

1. ____
2. ____
3. ____

Answers: 1. plain 2. plane 3. plane 4. plain 5. plane

pray / prey

Study these words to learn their differences.

*Previously Used Words
made
peace
pair
altar
grown
hare

1 **pray** - to talk to God

a. The priest made* it a point to **pray** for peace*.
b. In some countries people **pray** many times each day.
c. The middle-aged pair* started to **pray** in front of the altar*.

2 **prey** - unable to resist attack; victim

a. Grown* people many times fall **prey** to con artists.
b. The elderly are the favorite **prey** of criminals.
c. The careless hare* became the eagle's **prey**.

PRACTICE EXERCISES

Write the correct word in the blank space. (Answers at bottom.)

1. Even though he was going to die the convict refused to ________________.
2. Small animals are usually ________________ to larger ones.
3. "Will God hear me if I _____?" asked the little girl.
4. Do you ________________ everyday?
5. Homeless people often fall ________________ to street violence.

Write your own sentences.

1. ____
2. ____

Answers: 1. pray 2. prey 3. pray 4. pray 5. prey

principal / principle

Study these words to learn their differences.

*Previously Used Words
meet
our
mete
coarse
heel
made
sense

1 **principal** - a person or group in authority or leadership position

a. He is the **principal** owner of the company.
b. Her company is the **principal** donator to that charity.
c. My father didn't want to be the **principal** speaker.

2 **principal** - the director of an educational institution

a. Their high school **principal** wanted to meet* all the students.
b. Our* **principal** decided to mete* out strict punishment to the coarse* talking student.
c. As a **principal** he's nothing but a heel*.

3 **principle** - law; doctrine

a. The U.S. Constitution is the **principle** upon which the country is governed.
b. Most autocratic countries have no stated **principle** for governing.
c. The tyrant's **principle** of law made* no sense*.

PRACTICE EXERCISES

Write the correct word in the blank space. (Answers at bottom.)

1. Laurie is the ________________ owner of the company.
2. The basic ________________ of American democracy is the Constitution.
3. His ________________ of rule was sheer force.
4. She is the best ________________ in the school district.
5. The ________________ investor died.

Write your own sentences.

1. ____
2. ____
3. ____

Answers: 1. principal 2. principle 3. principle 4. principal 5. principal

SECTION TWO WORD REVIEW

Part A

DIRECTIONS: *Here are some of the new words covered in Section Two. Circle the one that fits best.*

1. The (principal, principle) of our school is very strict.
2. Mary's group reached the (peak, peek, pique) of the mountain first.
3. The mother did the homework (for, four, fore) her son.
4. Our team (won, one) the race.
5. Many people (pray, prey) everyday.
6. The (hall, haul) was long and narrow.
7. The robber broke the (pane, pain) of glass with a hammer.
8. The man was (hoarse, horse) and couldn't sing the hymn.
9. Everyone had a (marry, merry) time at the party.
10. Both the youths had a (hostile, hostel) attitude.
11. Their (made, maid) doesn't work on weekends.
12. Her little boy ate the (hole, whole) box of cookies.
13. Let's (meat, meet, mete) in the afternoon at the station.
14. His brother looked weak and (pail, pale) after the marathon.
15. I've had the (flew, flu, flue) for a week.
16. He doesn't (hear, here) very well.
17. We took the (plain, plane) from New York to Los Angeles.
18. I thought you (gnu, knew, new) her.
19. She used white (flour, flower) to bake the cake.
20. The injured dog began to (groan, grown).

SECTION TWO WORD REVIEW

Part B

DIRECTIONS: *Match the words with their definitions. Write the letter in front of the word.*

____ 1. know	a. a symbol of worship
____ 2. hour	b. a song of praise or joy
____ 3. hare	c. to make better; to get well
____ 4. mail	d. string tied in a lump
____ 5. inn	e. something used to hang clothes on
____ 6. hymn	f. to run away from danger
____ 7. peace	g. letters
____ 8. heal	h. equal to 60 minutes
____ 9. prey	i. fruit
____ 10. idol	j. a place where travelers eat and sleep
____ 11. lone	k. not at war
____ 12. night	l. to perceive correctly; to understand
____ 13. plain	m. to have done something
____ 14. made	n. victim
____ 15. flee	o. a furry animal that looks like a rabbit
____ 16. pear	p. law
____ 17. hanger	q. no sunlight; dark
____ 18. principle	r. undecorated
____ 19. knot	s. express grief over a death
____ 20. mourning	t. having no company

SECTION TWO WORD REVIEW

Part C

DIRECTIONS: Circle Right or Wrong for the proper usage of each bold word in the following sentences.

1. Alice has the **flew**. Right / Wrong
2. **Four** couples came to the party. Right / Wrong
3. The injured dog started to **groan**. Right / Wrong
4. The **ferry** was crowded with passengers. Right / Wrong
5. Many people were waiting in the **hall**. Right / Wrong
6. She likes **hymn** very much. Right / Wrong
7. Every **flour** in the garden was a different color. Right / Wrong
8. That team doesn't play **fare**. Right / Wrong
9. Janet rode the **hoarse** through the park. Right / Wrong
10. Our pilot parked the plane in the **hanger**. Right / Wrong
11. Alex bought his wife a **fir** coat. Right / Wrong
12. We dug a big **hole** in the ground. Right / Wrong
13. It was cheap to stay in the **hostel**. Right / Wrong
14. My neighbors took out a **lone** on their house. Right / Wrong
15. That butcher has very tender **meet**. Right / Wrong
16. After the long hike both my **feet** hurt. Right / Wrong
17. A **heard** of cattle could be seen in the distance. Right / Wrong
18. It started to **hail** during our picnic. Right / Wrong
19. All the soldiers began to **flea** the battlefield. Right / Wrong
20. We could see the rescue **flair** from the sky. Right / Wrong

SECTION THREE

rain / reign / rein

Study these words to learn their differences.

*Previously Used Words
been
for
hour
horse
knight
one

1 **rain** - water falling from the sky

a. The **rain** has been* coming down for* an hour*.
b. Many parts of California get very little **rain**.
c. I think it's going to **rain**.

2 **reign** - the domination or power of a ruler

a. Queen Victoria's **reign** lasted for 63 years.
b. Some rulers **reign** with an iron fist.
c. The Pope's **reign** lasted less than two weeks.

3 **rein** - a strap or rope by which a person controls an animal

a. The left **rein** broke as the rider pulled back to stop the horse*.
b. The knight* fell off and held on to only one* **rein**.
c. The blacksmith patched the **rein** with glue.

Note: Many times the above word is used in the plural, *reins*. Example: He pulled up on the *reins* of the camel.

PRACTICE EXERCISES

✎ *Write the correct word in the blank space. (Answers at bottom.)*

1. Her ________________ was the longest in history.
2. At noon it started to ________________.
3. The country has lived under military ________________ for 100 years.
4. The ________________ broke when the horse suddenly jumped.
5. Last night the weather forecaster predicted ________________ for today.

✎ *Write your own sentences.*

1. ____
2. ____
3. ____

Answers: 1. reign 2. rain 3. reign 4. rein 5. rain

read / red

Study these words to learn their differences.

1 **read** - past tense of read; to have understood or attempted to understand something that is printed or written

a. I **read** the magazine ad* last night.*
b. They **read** the story but thought it was a bore*.
c. I **read** the thesis but did not* understand a word of it.

Note: The present tense of *read* is also spelled *read*, but pronounced differently. Example: *Read* the book now. Check your dictionary for details.

2 **red** - the color red

a. Both the French and American flags are **red**, white, and blue.
b. They were all merry* and had **red** faces.
c. You are supposed to drink **red** wine with meat*.

3 **red** - showing an economic loss

a. All I have to show for* my company is **red** ink.
b. "In* the **red**" is the opposite of "in* the black."
c. Deficit spending is always in* the **red**.

Note: Many times this usage of *red* includes the words *in the* preceding *red*.

***Previously Used Words**

ad
night
bore
not
merry
meat
for
in

PRACTICE EXERCISES

Write the correct word in the blank space. (Answers at bottom.)

1. I ________________ the report yesterday.
2. His favorite color is ________________.
3. Their company slipped into the ________________ this past month.
4. Cindy ________________ many books while in college.
5. Most government run industries are in the ________________.

Write your own sentences.

1. ____
2. ____
3. ____

Answers: 1. read 2. red 3. red 4. read 5. red

read / reed

Study these words to learn their differences.

1 **read** – to understand letters or symbols; to learn, or attempt to learn, from written or printed matter.

a. She started to **read** when she was four*.
b. My aunt* used to **read** to me when I was a child.
c. I try to **read** one* book a month.

2 **reed** – any variety of tall grass with slender, jointed stems that grows mainly in wet regions

a. Many scientists believe that the first straw was actually a **reed**.
b. The bee* crawled to the top of the **reed**, then flew* away.
c. Many woodwind instruments have a **reed** attached to the mouthpiece.

***Previously Used Words**

four
aunt
one
bee
flew

PRACTICE EXERCISES

Write the correct word in the blank space. (Answers at bottom.)

1. The guide showed us how to use a __________________ for drinking water.
2. I don't want to __________________ the newspaper.
3. A single __________________ was floating in the river.
4. Do you like to __________________?
5. The __________________ was tall and green.

Write your own sentences.

1. ____
2. ____

Answers: 1. reed 2. read 3. reed 4. read 5. reed

right / rite / write

Study these words to learn their differences.

*Previously Used Words
idle
knew
not
knot
mail
in
one
principle
marry
hostile
maid
here
be
pale
plane
flew
pair
morning
principal

1 **right** - true; correct

a. Since he didn't set the idle* **right** the engine ran too fast.
b. The information he gave me was not* **right**.
c. She knew* the **right** way to tie the knot*.

2 **right** - the right side; opposite of left

a. He dropped the mail* in* the slot with his **right** hand.
b. My house is on the **right** side of the road.
c. Turn **right** at the next corner.

3 **right** - something that is properly due to a person or people

a. Many people in* the world today are denied the **right** to vote.
b. One* principle* of American freedom is that every person has the **right** of free speech.
c. "It's my **right** to marry* anyone I choose!" declared the hostile* daughter.

4 **right** - conservative party or political movement; conservative belief

a. That congressman is a member of the **right** wing.
b. Most people on the **right** are conservative in* their views.
c. The **Right** and Left are always fighting with each other.

Note: Many times capital letters are used for *Right* and *Left* when referring to political parties or groups.

5 **right** - to designate immediate action

a. "I'll do it **right** away," promised the maid*.
b. "Come here* **right** now!" demanded his mother.
c. It must be* done **right** this very minute.

6 **right** - to designate immediate position or location; exact time

a. The hijacker with a pale* face sat **right** next to me.
b. The plane* flew* **right** overhead.
c. Most Japanese trains, subways, and buses are **right** on time.

7 **rite** - a ceremony

a. The religious **rite** was interesting to watch.
b. The **rite** of passage into the fraternity was complicated.
c. The pair* passed the group's **rite** with flying colors.

right / rite / write

8 **write** – to spell and compose

a. Some American high school graduates cannot read or **write**.
b. My father-in-law likes to **write** letters in* the morning*.
c. I try to **write** my former principal* once a year.

PRACTICE EXERCISES

Write the correct word in the blank space. (Answers at bottom.)

1. None of his answers were ________________.
2. The marriage ________________ took only 10 minutes.
3. Let's go ________________ now.
4. She promised to ________________ me a letter.
5. All the students raised their ________________ hands.

Write your own sentences.

1. ____
2. ____
3. ____
4. ____
5. ____
6. ____
7. ____
8. ____

Answers: **1. right 2. rite 3. right 4. write 5. right**

road / rode / rowed

Study these words to learn their differences.

1 **road** - route; highway; street

a. Look both ways before you cross the **road**.
b. The **road** was a dead end.
c. Every **road** on the course* was narrow and bumpy.

2 **rode** - past tense of ride

a. The boy **rode** the horse* around the hostel*.
b. Everybody **rode** in* one* car.
c. Shane **rode** off into the sunset.

3 **rowed** - past tense of row; to have moved a boat with oars

a. She **rowed** the boat across the river to peek* at her idol*.
b. The young boy **rowed** the canoe with great difficulty.
c. In ancient times, battleships were **rowed** by* male* slaves.

***Previously Used Words**

course
horse
hostel
in
one
peek
idol
by
male

PRACTICE EXERCISES

Write the correct word in the blank space. (Answers at bottom.)

1. We took the dirt ____________ to town.
2. Their team ____________ the boat to victory.
3. I ____________ a motorcycle in the race.
4. Every ____________ was closed.
5. He ____________ until his arms ached.

Write your own sentences.

1. ____
2. ____
3. ____

Answers: 1. road 2. rowed 3. rode 4. road 5. rowed

roe / row

Study these words to learn their differences.

*Previously Used Words
for
not
made
one
plain
in

1 **roe** – fish eggs, especially still inside the fish

a. Many people love to eat raw salmon **roe**.
b. A lot of American fishermen use salmon **roe** for* bait.
c. Sometimes I eat herring **roe** on crackers.

2 **row** – to move a boat with oars

a. It is not* easy to **row** against a river current.
b. My wife could not* **row** the boat.
c. The team started to **row** past their opponents.

3 **row** – a line of objects, things, or people

a. Every **row** the farmer made* was as straight as an arrow.
b. The baker had only one* **row** of plain* cookies.
c. All the participants stood in* a **row**.

PRACTICE EXERCISES

Write the correct word in the blank space. (Answers at bottom.)

1. The ________________ of tables was not straight.
2. He was too small to ________________ the boat.
3. All the workers stood in a ________________.
4. That ________________ was delicious.
5. "Can you teach me how to ________________?" asked the girl.

Write your own sentences.

1. ____
2. ____
3. ____

Answers: 1. row 2. row 3. row 4. roe 5. row

role / roll

Study these words to learn their differences.

1 **role** – a part played by an actor or actress

a. Who played the **role** of the villain?
b. I knew* she wouldn't accept that **role**.
c. My brother played the **role** of a father in* mourning*.

2 **roll** – list of names of students, members, participants, etc.

a. Please add* his name to the **roll**.
b. As Professor Smith started to call **roll** it began to hail*.
c. The **roll** had too many students on it.

3 **roll** – to move by turning over and over

a. The workers began to **roll** the carpet onto the den floor.
b. Greg told his dog to **roll** over.
c. The red* bowling ball* started to **roll** down the alley.

Note: To *roll out the carpet* or *roll out the red carpet* means to give someone very special treatment. Example: The government decided to *roll out the red carpet* for the visiting dignitaries.

4 **roll** – a sweet pastry

a. The rotund man ate* a jelly **roll** for breakfast every morning*.
b. The customer ordered eight* donuts and one* giant chocolate **roll**.
c. The baker always gave the little girl a free **roll**.

***Previously Used Words**

knew
in
mourning
add
hail
red
ball
ate
morning
eight
one

PRACTICE EXERCISES

Write the correct word in the blank space. (Answers at bottom.)

1. A ________________ is not good for my diet.
2. John didn't like his ________________ in the play.
3. The trainer made his dog ________________ over.
4. The teacher hated calling ________________.
5. How much is that plain ________________?

Write your own sentences.

1. ____
2. ____
3. ____
4. ____

Answers: 1. roll 2. role 3. roll 4. roll 5. roll

rote / wrote

Study these words to learn their differences.

*Previously Used Words
by
aunt
mail
idyll

1 **rote** - to commit to memory with little or no intelligence involved

a. A lot of education systems are only concerned with **rote** memorization.
b. To pass some tests it is necessary to study by* **rote**.
c. Most American students don't learn by* **rote**.

2 **wrote** - past tense of write; to have spelled and composed

a. Last week I **wrote** my aunt* a letter but I forgot to mail* it.
b. Shakespeare **wrote** many famous plays.
c. My roommate **wrote** an award-winning idyll* about life in Scotland.

PRACTICE EXERCISES

Write the correct word in the blank space. (Answers at bottom.)

1. Most students in Japan learn by __________________.
2. I __________________ them a letter yesterday.
3. Who __________________ this letter?
4. We had to study by __________________ to pass the test.
5. Sally __________________ a letter to the magazine.

Write your own sentences.

1. ____
2. ____

Answers: 1. rote 2. wrote 3. wrote 4. rote 5. wrote

sail / sale

Study these words to learn their differences.

*Previously Used Words
one
read
our
isle
new
blew
not
for
made
ad
red

1 **sail** - a fabric by which a boat or ship is driven

a. The small boat had only one* **sail.**
b. The captain ordered the sailors to raise the **sail.**
c. We had to sew the **sail** with nylon thread.

2 **sail** - to guide or captain a vessel

a. I read* a book on how to **sail.**
b. Our* plan is to learn how to **sail** a boat.
c. The captain tried to **sail** the ship away from the rocky isle*.

3 **sale** - the act of selling something

a. The new* representative blew* the **sale.**
b. The house was not* for* **sale.**
c. He hasn't made* a **sale** all month.

4 **sale** - bargain

a. When they have a **sale** they write the ad* in big red* letters.
b. I saved a lot of money at the year end **sale.**
c. The store had a half price **sale.**

PRACTICE EXERCISES

Write the correct word in the blank space. (Answers at bottom.)

1. Everything in the store was on ________________.
2. I am learning how to ________________.
3. She made a ________________ in her first week.
4. The ________________ was made of nylon.
5. She spent all her money at the supermarket ________________.

Write your own sentences.

1. ____
2. ____
3. ____
4. ____

Answers: 1. sale 2. sail 3. sale 4. sail 5. sale

scene / seen

Study these words to learn their differences.

1 **scene** - a single part of a play or movie

a. The last **scene** in* *Gone with the Wind* is very famous.
b. The idol* has a small cameo part during the second **scene**.
c. Our* director thought we did the **scene** just right*.

2 **scene** - an embarrassing or unpleasant situation

a. The child started to bawl* in the store, causing a **scene**.
b. John's arrogant father started to cause a **scene** when the waiter brought him* the wrong order.
c. It is best not* to make a **scene** in public.

3 **seen** - past participle of see; to have looked at or perceived with the eyes

a. That was the best fair* I've ever **seen**.
b. I have never **seen** a hare* run so fast.
c. This is the first time I have **seen** it rain* from morning* to night*.

***Previously Used Words**

in
idol
our
right
bawl
him
not
fair
hare
rain
morning
night

PRACTICE EXERCISES

Write the correct word in the blank space. (Answers at bottom.)

1. The first ________________ in the movie was boring.
2. That was the best baseball game I have ever ________________.
3. The ambassador started to cause a ________________.
4. He had never ________________ so many people before.
5. The actress wanted to do the ________________ over.

Write your own sentences.

1. ____
2. ____
3. ____

Answers: 1. scene 2. seen 3. scene 4. seen 5. scene

sea / see

Study these words to learn their differences.

*Previously Used Words
in

1 **sea** – a large body of salt water; ocean

a. All the crewmen were lost at **sea**.
b. The Mediterranean **Sea** has many beautiful beaches.
c. Let's walk to the **sea** and go swimming.

2 **see** – to look at or perceive with the eye

a. On a clear day you can **see** for miles.
b. Someday I want to **see** Mt. Everest.
c. "Did you **see** them yesterday?" asked the detective.

3 **see** – to understand; to agree with

a. I **see** what you mean.
b. He doesn't **see** it my way.
c. I can't **see** any point in* raising the price.

PRACTICE EXERCISES

Write the correct word in the blank space. (Answers at bottom.)

1. They don't want to ________________ each other anymore.
2. The ________________ was calm and blue.
3. I don't think you ________________ what I mean.
4. "I can't ________________ the stage," complained the man in the rear.
5. The ________________ is always crowded during summertime.

Write your own sentences.

1. ____
2. ____
3. ____

Answers: 1. see 2. sea 3. see 4. see 5. sea

seam / seem

Study these words to learn their differences.

1 **seam** - where two pieces of material are stitched or sewn together

a. The rough road* made* me split a **seam** in* my pants.
b. His suit had a double **seam**.
c. My wife had to repair the **seam** of her skirt with an old piece* of cloth.

2 **seem** - to give an impression; to appear

a. He doesn't **seem** to enjoy studying English.
b. The hound doesn't **seem** to know* the scent*.
c. They **seem** to be* having a good time.

***Previously Used Words**

road
made
in
piece
know
scent
be

PRACTICE EXERCISES

✎ *Write the correct word in the blank space. (Answers at bottom.)*

1. The ________________ on the shirt was not very strong.
2. He doesn't ________________ to be happy.
3. This plan doesn't ________________ to be working well.
4. Can you repair this torn ________________?
5. They don't ________________ to be interested.

✎ *Write your own sentences.*

1. ____
2. ____

Answers: 1. seam 2. seem 3. seem 4. seam 5. seem

Seoul / sole / soul

Study these words to learn their differences.

1 **Seoul** – the capital of South Korea

a. The night* lights in* **Seoul** are exciting.
b. There are daily flights from Tokyo to **Seoul**.
c. Her daughter graduated from the University of **Seoul**.

2 **sole** – the underneath part of a foot or shoe

a. The **sole** on my right* shoe has a hole* in* it.
b. The **sole** was made* of leather.
c. This **sole** needs repair, but the heel* is fine.

3 **sole** – any type of flatfish

a. She likes fillet of **sole** and salmon roe*.
b. The **sole** they served at the inn* was delicious.
c. French style **sole** has a unique taste.

4 **soul** – the essence of life; the spiritual principle in human beings

a. Most people believe in* the principle* of a human **soul**.
b. Christianity believes that every person has a **soul**.
c. The devil bargained for* Daniel Webster's **soul**.

Note: Many people call some types of music performed by African-Americans *soul music*.
Example: He loves to listen to *soul music*.

***Previously Used Words**

night
in
right
hole
made
heel
roe
inn
principle
for

PRACTICE EXERCISES

Write the correct word in the blank space. (Answers at bottom.)

1. He would have traded his ________________ for the contract.
2. The fillet of ________________ at that restaurant is excellent.
3. Our minister always speaks about his trip to ________________.
4. The ________________ of my left shoe is worn all the way through.
5. The ________________ was baked and covered with chili sauce.

Write your own sentences.

1. ______________________________
2. ______________________________
3. ______________________________
4. ______________________________

Answers: 1. soul 2. sole 3. Seoul 4. sole 5. sole

sew / so / sow

Study these words to learn their differences.

1 **sew** – to put together by stitching

a. My wife is going to **sew** a seam* into her blouse.
b. He decided to **sew** the torn jacket himself.
c. These days many girls can't **sew**.

2 **so** – therefore

a. The news predicted rain*, **so** we didn't go to the sea*.
b. She gave the right* answer, **so** the principal* was happy.
c. He caught the flu* and is hoarse*, **so** he can't sing the hymn*.

3 **sow** – to plant seeds, usually by hand; to spread ideas

a. Many years ago farmers used to **sow** seeds by* hand.
b. My father decided to **sow** the front lawn.
c. What she wrote* began to **sow** the seeds of discontent.

Note: The word *sow* also means a female pig but is pronounced differently. Check your dictionary for details.

***Previously Used Words**

seam
rain
sea
right
principal
flu
hoarse
hymn
by
wrote

PRACTICE EXERCISES

Write the correct word in the blank space. (Answers at bottom.)

1. He can ________________ very well.
2. The old farmer would always ________________ his fields by hand.
3. They don't have any time, ________________ they can't come.
4. The radicals tried to ________________ rebellion among the workers.
5. He didn't pass the final, ________________ he couldn't graduate.

Write your own sentences.

1. ____
2. ____
3. ____

Answers: 1. sew 2. sow 3. so 4. sow 5. so

soar / sore

Study these words to learn their differences.

***Previously Used Words**
in
new
him
one
for
heal

1 **soar** – to fly high in the air, usually without engine power

a. It was thrilling to see the eagle **soar** in* the sky.
b. The glider began to **soar** above the clouds.
c. The kite wouldn't **soar** in* the light wind.

2 **soar** – to rise dramatically

a. Her popularity started to **soar** after the election.
b. Prices began to **soar** during the oil crisis.
c. With inflation the prices of new* houses started to **soar**.

3 **sore** – causing pain; hurt

a. I have a **sore** throat.
b. His **sore** back always bothers him*.
c. My muscles were **sore** from too much jogging.

4 **sore** – torn or ruptured skin that is usually infected; ulcer; boil

a. The **sore** on the animal's leg was infected.
b. Her doctor put some medicine on the **sore**.
c. It took one* week for* the **sore** to heal*.

PRACTICE EXERCISES

Write the correct word in the blank space. (Answers at bottom.)

1. The small company's profits started to ________________.
2. He put some ointment on the ________________.
3. The huge bird began to ________________ above the hills.
4. My elbow is ________________.
5. My trainer massaged my ________________ muscles.

Write your own sentences.

1. ____
2. ____
3. ____
4. ____

Answers: 1. soar 2. sore 3. soar 4. sore 5. sore

son / sun

Study these words to learn their differences.

*Previously Used Words
rowed
sell
sensor
sew
fore

1 **son** - a male offspring

a. His **son** sat next to him as he rowed* the boat.
b. Their **son** decided to sell* his electric sensor*.
c. She taught her **son** how to sew.*

2 **sun** - the star nearest the earth that all other planets revolve around and receive their heat from

a. The **sun** is nearly 93,000,000 miles (150,000,000 kilometers) away from the earth.
b. Copernicus was the first to believe that the earth revolves around the **sun**.
c. Some day solar power from the **sun** will come to the fore*.

PRACTICE EXERCISES

Write the correct word in the blank space. (Answers at bottom.)

1. Her ________________ became a famous lawyer.
2. Many early civilizations used to worship the ________________.
3. They have two daughters and a ________________.
4. My neighbor likes to lay out in the ________________ all day long.
5. Their ________________ went to South America.

Write your own sentences.

1. ____
2. ____

Answers: 1. son 2. sun 3. son 4. sun 5. son

stair / stare

Study these words to learn their differences.

*Previously Used Words
bye
son
sight
prey
pale
do

1 **stair** - one of many steps going up or down

a. "Be careful," warned Richard, "the last **stair** is broken."
b. She repaired the damaged **stair,** but the wood didn't match.
c. "Bye,"* called out her boyfriend as he reached the bottom **stair**.

Note: The above word is many times used in the plural, *stairs*. Example: He walked up the *stairs* to the library. Also, *stairway* is often used to mean *stairs*.

2 **stare** - to look at something or someone with fixed, wide open eyes

a. My son* began to **stare** at the sight* of the prey* between the lion's jaws.
b. Her face became pale* and all she could do* was **stare**.
c. Bob couldn't help but **stare** at the beautiful woman.

PRACTICE EXERCISES

Write the correct word in the blank space. (Answers at bottom.)

1. A _______________ in the middle of the stairway is loose.
2. It is not polite to _______________ at people.
3. His cold _______________ began to frighten the children.
4. They painted each _______________ a different color.
5. The candidate could only _______________ at the unfriendly audience.

Write your own sentences.

1. ____
2. ____

Answers: 1. stair 2. stare 3. stare 4. stair 5. stare

stake / steak

Study these words to learn their differences.

*Previously Used Words
row
damn
see
in
coarse
sale

1 **stake** – something driven into the ground as a marker or to hold something down

a. The wooden **stake** marked the beginning of the first row*.
b. "I tripped over the damn* **stake** because I didn't see* it," retorted the angry tourist.
c. The camper drove in* the last **stake** of the tent.

2 **stake** – something that is gained or lost during an argument, confrontation, battle, fight, etc.

a. During the Second World War freedom was at **stake**.
b. Only pride was at **stake** during the fight.
c. The gambler put his house at **stake** during the game.

3 **steak** – a slice of meat or fish

a. The texture of the T-bone **steak** was very coarse*.
b. Filet mignon **steak** is tender and quite expensive.
c. The store had a sale* on **steak**.

PRACTICE EXERCISES

Write the correct word in the blank space. (Answers at bottom.)

1. He always likes his ________________ rare.
2. The championship was at ________________ during the game.
3. Since he was a vegetarian he didn't order ________________.
4. The metal ________________ marked the boundary of our land.
5. The politician's good name was at ________________.

Write your own sentences.

1. ____
2. ____
3. ____

Answers: 1. steak 2. stake 3. steak 4. stake 5. stake

steal / steel

Study these words to learn their differences.

1 **steal** - to wrongfully take something without permission

a. "Thou shalt not* **steal**" is one* of the Ten Commandments.
b. He was planning to **steal** his friend's money.
c. The child didn't want to **steal** the candy.

2 **steal** - bargain; exceptionally good purchase price

a. The antique was a **steal** at the closing sale*.
b. She got a **steal** on that car.
c. "It was a **steal**," proclaimed the merry* customer.

3 **steel** - commercial iron; a metal

a. "This building is **steel** reinforced," said the real estate agent.
b. His **steel** sword was razor sharp.
c. The stake* was made* of **steel**.

***Previously Used Words**

not
one
sale
merry
stake
made

PRACTICE EXERCISES

Write the correct word in the blank space. (Answers at bottom.)

1. He tried to convince his friend to ________________ the cigarettes.
2. That country's major export is ________________.
3. My nephew got a ________________ at the garage sale.
4. It is not a good idea to ________________ things.
5. The new car had plastic, not ________________ bumpers.

Write your own sentences.

1. ____
2. ____
3. ____

Answers: 1. steal 2. steel 3. steal 4. steal 5. steel

suite / sweet

Study these words to learn their differences.

***Previously Used Words**
steak
in
maid
scent

1 **suite** - a group of rooms in a hotel connected to each other

a. They had steak* and eggs in* their bridal **suite**.
b. We tried to rent the executive **suite** but it was already occupied.
c. The maid* took all day to clean the **suite**.

Note: The word suite and suit are not pronounced the same. Check your dictionary for the proper pronunciation.

2 **sweet** - not bitter, salty, or sour; sugary

a. My husband likes to drink **sweet** wine.
b. The chocolate malt was very **sweet**.
c. The scent* of **sweet** candy filled the shop.

PRACTICE EXERCISES

Write the correct word in the blank space. (Answers at bottom.)

1. The ice tea was too __________________.
2. The hotel __________________ overlooked the entire city.
3. I like salty, not __________________ things.
4. Their wedding cake was not very __________________.
5. Our __________________ was big and comfortable.

Write your own sentences.

1. ____
2. ____

Answers: 1. sweet 2. suite 3. sweet 4. sweet 5. suite

tail / tale

Study these words to learn their differences.

*Previously Used Words
our
stair
in
be

1 **tail** - the tubular portion of an animal's rear end

a. Our* dog's **tail** began banging the bottom stair*.
b. A whale's **tail** is very powerful.
c. The elephant had a rather short **tail**.

2 **tail** - to the rear; to the end

a. The marathon runner was in* the **tail** of the group.
b. Bill always brings up the **tail** of late students.
c. "Try not to always be* at the **tail** when hiking," advised the guide.

3 **tale** - story

a. Charles Dickens wrote *A Tale of Two Cities*.
b. The excuse he gave sounded like a tall **tale**.
c. She can really tell a good **tale**.

PRACTICE EXERCISES

✎ *Write the correct word in the blank space. (Answers at bottom.)*

1. The dog got its ________________ caught in the door.
2. His fishing ________________ wasn't the truth.
3. Kelly brought up the ________________ of the marathon.
4. A kangaroo uses its ________________ for balance.
5. No one believed the ________________ he was telling.

✎ *Write your own sentences.*

1. ____
2. ____
3. ____

Answers: 1. tail 2. tale 3. tail 4. tail 5. tale

their / there / they're

Study these words to learn their differences.

1 **their** - relating to them

a. That is **their** berth*.
b. **Their** scene* was filmed in* a hotel suite* with the sun* shining through a single pane* of glass.
c. I rode* to **their** house last night* on my horse*.

2 **there** - certain place or location

a. The site* of the new* capitol* building will be* right* **there**.
b. I sent* the package **there** yesterday.
c. Put your books down **there** and have a seat.

3 **they're** - they are

a. **They're** not* paying the taxi fare*.
b. **They're** going to pray* for* his soul*.
c. "What do you think **they're** doing in* the company?" asked the suspicious detective.

***Previously Used Words**

berth
scene
in
suite
sun
pane
rode
night
horse
site
new
capitol
be
right
sent
not
fare
pray
for
soul

PRACTICE EXERCISES

Write the correct word in the blank space. (Answers at bottom.)

1. I think that is ________________ airplane.
2. Let's go ________________ tomorrow.
3. ________________ really nice people.
4. Do you remember ________________ telephone number?
5. I don't think ________________ home.

Write your own sentences.

1. ____
2. ____
3. ____

Answers: 1. their 2. there 3. They're 4. their 5. they're

threw / through

Study these words to learn their differences.

1 **threw** – past tense of throw; to have propelled something through the air

a. He **threw** the pear* to his girlfriend.
b. Jack tried to steal* second base* but the pitcher **threw** him* out.
c. After she wrote* the letter she tore it up and **threw** it away.

2 **through** – a function word used to go into and out of something or someone

a. The bullet went **through** the soldier's arm.
b. Larry made his dog jump **through** the hoop.
c. The burglar tried to peek* **through** the hole* but couldn't see* anything.

Note: This word can also be spelled *thru*, with the same pronunciation and meaning; however, this is considered an abbreviated form of the word and is not proper usage.

3 **through** – to be done; to be finished; completed

a. The waiter took my plate before I was **through** eating.
b. I'm not* **through** working yet.
c. I can't get **through** in* time.

***Previously Used Words**

pear
steal
base
him
wrote
peek
hole
see
not
in

PRACTICE EXERCISES

Write the correct word in the blank space. (Answers at bottom.)

1. Janet ________________ the discus to a new world record.
2. The epidemic went ________________ the whole village.
3. I'm not ________________ with that report yet.
4. The lottery winner ________________ the money up in the air.
5. Their excited child kept running ________________ the room.

Write your own sentences.

1. ____
2. ____
3. ____

Answers: 1. threw 2. through 3. through 4. threw 5. through

to / too / two

Study these words to learn their differences.

1 **to** - going toward something; in the direction

a. This road* leads **to** the capitol*.
b. I'm going **to** go **to** their* house through* the forest.
c. She went **to** the steel* mill early this morning*.

2 **too** - also

a. "I want to* go, **too**!" bellowed the child.
b. He has a pain* in* his heel,* **too**.
c. "Me, **too**!" exclaimed the girl with an excited stare*.

3 **too** - excessive; in excess

a. I think this candy is **too** sweet*.
b. "You've said 'damn*' one* **too** many times," scolded her aunt*.
c. **Too** much alcohol is bad for* your health.

4 **two** - the number; 2

a. **Two** deer* ran across the road*.
b. The **two** men tried to* reign* the country without a fair* principle* of law.
c. The last **two** cars brought up the tail* of the race.

***Previously Used Words**

road
capitol
their
through
steel
morning
to
pain
in
heel
stare
sweet
damn
one
aunt
for
deer
reign
fair
principle
tail

PRACTICE EXERCISES

✎ *Write the correct word in the blank space. (Answers at bottom.)*

1. The ________________ men began fighting.
2. I had a good time, ________________.
3. This place is ________________ cold to live in winter.
4. Let's go ________________ the movies.
5. The town is ________________ far out in the desert.

✎ *Write your own sentences.*

1. ____
2. ____
3. ____
4. ____

Answers: 1. two 2. too 3. too 4. to 5. too

toe / tow

Study these words to learn their differences.

1 **toe** – one of the terminal members on the front end of a foot

a. I sprained my **toe** playing soccer.
b. His broken **toe** will take two* months to* heal*.
c. She jammed her **toe** when she kicked the ball*.

Note: The biggest toe on a person's foot is called the ***big toe***. The next three toes are called the ***middle toes***. The smallest toe is called the ***little*** or ***baby toe***.

2 **tow** – to pull or drag behind

a. Do* you think you can **tow** that piece* of steel* by* yourself?
b. They're* going to* **tow** the boat up river.
c. The police called a truck to* **tow** the car away.

Note: A truck that hauls cars or trucks away is called a *tow truck*.

***Previously Used Words**

two
to
heal
ball
do
piece
steel
by
they're

PRACTICE EXERCISES

Write the correct word in the blank space. (Answers at bottom.)

1. We couldn't ________________ the truck uphill.
2. My big ________________ hurts.
3. The men started to ________________ the car to the repair shop.
4. The monkey's ________________ was bleeding.
5. It costs a lot of money to ________________ a large truck.

Write your own sentences.

1. ____
2. ____

Answers: 1. tow 2. toe 3. tow 4. toe 5. tow

vain / vane / vein

Study these words to learn their differences.

*Previously Used Words
made
their
rote
in
for
to
stare
no
one
him
too
seem
so
blue
red
pare
tail

1 **vain** - futile; useless

a. He made* a **vain** attempt at making an excuse.
b. All their* rote* study was in* **vain**.
c. Her **vain** cries for* help went unanswered.

2 **vain** - excessive self pride; conceited

a. **Vain** people like everybody to* stare* at them.
b. No* one* liked him* because he was too* **vain**.
c. "Why does she seem* so* **vain**?" wondered Mary.

3 **vane** - a device used to show the direction of wind

a. Our neighbor's house has a weather **vane** on the roof.
b. That politician is exactly like a weather **vane**.
c. They have a blue* weather **vane** on their* red* barn .

4 **vein** - tubular, branching blood vessel

a. The nurse injected medicine into his **vein**.
b. During surgery the doctor tried to* pare* back the **vein**.
c. Her cat had a broken blood **vein** in* its tail*.

PRACTICE EXERCISES

Write the correct word in the blank space. (Answers at bottom.)

1. His __________________ attempt at lying only caused more trouble.
2. I broke a blood __________________ in my hand.
3. The __________________ on top of the house broke in the storm.
4. Martin is a __________________ person.
5. All her planning was in __________________.

Write your own sentences.

1. ____
2. ____
3. ____
4. ____

Answers: 1. vain 2. vein 3. vane 4. vain 5. vain

vary / very

Study these words to learn their differences.

*Previously Used Words
to
ad
seen
so
bore
bass
hoarse
read
tale

1 **vary** - to be different; not the same

a. People's opinions tend to* **vary** depending on which ad* they have seen.*
b. You must **vary** your approach when dealing with children.
c. The professor never tried to* **vary** his lectures, so* they were a total bore*.

2 **very** - exceedingly; to a high degree

a. His bass* voice sounds **very** hoarse*.
b. The announcer sounded **very** excited.
c. As the woman read* the horrifying tale* the audience was **very** quiet.

PRACTICE EXERCISES

Write the correct word in the blank space. (Answers at bottom.)

1. The union group leader decided to ________________ his approach.
2. That family's rent is ________________ expensive.
3. Her father was ________________ upset.
4. He didn't want to ________________ his successful sales pitch.
5. The machine shop was ________________ noisy.

Write your own sentences.

1. ____
2. ____

Answers: 1. vary 2. very 3. very 4. vary 5. very

waist / waste

Study these words to learn their differences.

1 **waist** - the part of the body immediately above the hips

a. The **waist** size of the new* dress is just right*.
b. My belt couldn't fit around his **waist**.
c. "Can I measure my **waist** size?" asked the customer.

2 **waste** - useless material; trash; garbage; rubbish; junk

a. It is not* a good idea to* bury* nuclear **waste**.
b. The **waste** from the factory was dumped into the river.
c. They threw* the chemical **waste** in* the sea*.

3 **waste** - not using something efficiently

a. "Don't **waste** time!" scolded the teacher.
b. Many times rich people **waste** money.
c. It is wrong to* **waste** natural resources.

***Previously Used Words**

new
right
not
to
bury
threw
in
sea

PRACTICE EXERCISES

Write the correct word in the blank space. (Answers at bottom.)

1. We must not ________________ human resources.
2. As the strike lingered on the ________________ began to pile up.
3. My ________________ size has gotten bigger.
4. That company's ________________ is costing millions of dollars.
5. He tends to ________________ a lot of time.

Write your own sentences.

1. ____
2. ____
3. ____

Answers: 1. waste 2. waste 3. waist 4. waste 5. waste

wait / weight

Study these words to learn their differences.

1 **wait** - to stay in one place for awhile

a. I'll **wait** for* you in* front of their* house.
b. He said he would **wait** over there*.
c. Mr. Jones decided that he should **wait** until his wife came home.

2 **wait** - give time for something to take place

a. The businessman was impatient and didn't want to* **wait**.
b. She didn't **wait** for* an answer.
c. "Let's **wait** until tomorrow morning,*" suggested the vice president.

3 **weight** - amount of heaviness

a. The movie idol* knew* he had to* lose some **weight**.
b. If you want to* pique* the boss ask her about her **weight**.
c. The sail* is not* the right* **weight**.

***Previously Used Words**

for
in
their
there
to
morning
idol
knew
pique
sail
not
right

PRACTICE EXERCISES

Write the correct word in the blank space. (Answers at bottom.)

1. I need to lose some ________________.
2. She'll ________________ there for you.
3. We should ________________ until the weather clears.
4. The ________________ of the extra baggage sank the small boat.
5. I don't have time to ________________.

Write your own sentences.

1. ____
2. ____
3. ____

Answers: 1. weight 2. wait 3. wait 4. weight 5. wait

war / wore

Study these words to learn their differences.

1 **war** - struggle between opposing forces; opposite of peace

a. It was hard for* him* to* bear* the memories of the **war**.
b. The knight* was not* afraid of going to* **war**.
c. Every male* in* the country was forced to* fight the **war**.

2 **wore** - past tense of wear; to have put on clothes

a. She **wore** a jacket because it was very* cold.
b. Yesterday I **wore** my jogging shoes.
c. The two* of them **wore** the same dress to* the ball*.

***Previously Used Words**

for
him
to
bear
knight
not
male
in
very
two
ball

PRACTICE EXERCISES

Write the correct word in the blank space. (Answers at bottom.)

1. He __________________ a tuxedo to the concert.
2. The __________________ divided the nation.
3. I __________________ my Hawaiian shirt to the luau.
4. Last year she __________________ a black dress to the party.
5. Mostly children were killed in the __________________.

Write your own sentences.

1. ____
2. ____

Answers: 1. wore 2. war 3. wore 4. wore 5. war

ware / wear / where

Study these words to learn their differences.

*Previously Used Words
very
high
buy
new
to
for
so
vain
one
write
serial

1 **ware** - manufactured goods

a. Chinese copper **ware** is very* high* priced.
b. All the earthen**ware** in the store was handmade.
c. When I first saw lacquer **ware** I thought it was plastic.

Note: The above word is usually used in combination with another word. Example: China *ware*, silver*ware*, etc. However, this is not always the case. Example: The merchant sold his *ware* on the street. This word is also many times used in the plural *wares* to mean the same thing. Example: The vendor sold his *wares* in the park.

2 **wear** - to put on clothes

a. I must buy* something new* to* **wear** for* the party.
b. My sister is so* vain* that she won't **wear** the same blouse more than one* time.
c. He doesn't like to* **wear** a shirt and tie.

Note: The word *wear* can also be used to describe attrition or deterioration. Example: Without oil, machines *wear* out much faster. Example: Constant water on a stone will eventually *wear* it down. *Wore* and *worn*, the past and past participle forms of *wear*, can also be used this way.

3 **where** - a place, position, or direction

a. "Can you tell me **where** the restroom is, please?" inquired the man.
b. I don't know **where** they are going.
c. Do you know **where** I should write* the serial* number on this report?

Practice Exercises on next page.

ware / wear / where

PRACTICE EXERCISES

✎ *Write the correct word in the blank space. (Answers at bottom.)*

1. The young boy was hawking his ________________ on the sidewalk.
2. "________________ is the hotel?" asked the lost tourist.
3. Make sure to ________________ something warm.
4. The silver ________________ looked beautiful on the table.
5. I don't know ________________ the book is.

✎ *Write your own sentences.*

1. ____
2. ____
3. ____

Answers: 1. ware 2. Where 3. wear 4. ware 5. where

warn / worn

Study these words to learn their differences.

1 **warn** - to inform in advance of danger or trouble

a. **Warn** me if you see* him*.
b. The statesman tried to* **warn** the country of the coming war*.
c. Wave your hand so* you can **warn** her.

2 **worn** - past participle of wear; to have put on clothes

a. He has always **worn** that coat.
b. I have never **worn** a tuxedo.
c. She hasn't **worn** her new* dress because the waist* is too* large.

***Previously Used Words**

see
him
to
war
so
new
waist
too

PRACTICE EXERCISES

Write the correct word in the blank space. (Answers at bottom.)

1. We tried to ________________ him of the danger.
2. They have ________________ the same uniforms for 20 years.
3. Make sure you ________________ me if you see her coming.
4. My grandfather has never ________________ a hat.
5. The birds started to ________________ the flock of the approaching lion.

Write your own sentences.

1. ____
2. ____

Answers: 1. warn 2. worn 3. warn 4. worn 5. warn

weak / week

Study these words to learn their differences.

1 **weak** - lacking strength; not strong

a. The seam* on the new* dress was very* **weak**.
b. Mr. Abbott looked **weak** and tired.
c. Her child was too* **weak** to* wave.

2 **week** - seven days in a row

a. Next **week** her son* will wear* his new* pair* of shoes.
b. Let's not* waste* any time this **week**.
c. "Your rent was due* last **week**!" stammered the irate landlord.

***Previously Used Words**

seam
new
very
too
to
son
wear
pair
not
waste
due

PRACTICE EXERCISES

Write the correct word in the blank space. (Answers at bottom.)

1. It took us one ________________ to prepare for the presentation.
2. Next ________________ I am going to Hong Kong.
3. He was very ________________ after the accident.
4. Your report was due last ________________.
5. She's too ________________ to move.

Write your own sentences.

1. ____
2. ____

Answers: 1. week 2. week 3. weak 4. week 5. weak

weather / whether

Study these words to learn their differences.

1 **weather** - condition of the atmosphere

a. The **weather** there* last week* was warm and dry.
b. Sometimes New York has very* bad **weather**.
c. I think we should wait* for* better **weather**.

2 **whether** - an alternative to possibilities or conditions

a. I don't know **whether** they're* home or at their* parents house.
b. **Whether** you like it or not*, you must do* your homework.
c. She doesn't know* **whether** they went to* the show or the restaurant.

***Previously Used Words**

there
week
very
wait
for
they're
their
not
do
know
to

PRACTICE EXERCISES

Write the correct word in the blank space. (Answers at bottom.)

1. ________________ you go or not is up to you.
2. The ________________ in New Zealand during summer is beautiful.
3. I don't know ________________ they are coming this week or next.
4. The ________________ doesn't look very good.
5. He doesn't know ________________ he passed or failed the exam.

Write your own sentences.

1. ____
2. ____

Answers: 1. Whether 2. weather 3. whether 4. weather
5. whether

which / witch

Study these words to learn their differences.

1 **which** – one of a group

a. **Which** honeymoon suite* do* you like best?
b. **Which** one* of you will weigh more after the pie eating contest?
c. Rick couldn't decide **which** present he liked best.

2 **witch** – a woman with supernatural powers; sorceress

a. The **witch** flew away on a broom.
b. The old **witch** didn't know* where* the two* little children went.
c. She dressed up like a **witch** for* the Halloween ball*.

3 **witch** – a despiteful woman

a. She is a real **witch**.
b. Our next door neighbor is a **witch**.
c. His wife turned out to* be* a **witch**.

Note: This usage is considered distasteful and should be avoided.

***Previously Used Words**

suite
do
one
know
where
two
for
ball
to
be

PRACTICE EXERCISES

Write the correct word in the blank space. (Answers at bottom.)

1. ________________ movie did you like best?
2. Sometimes she can be a real ________________.
3. The ________________ had a wide-brimmed, black hat.
4. ________________ team do you belong to?
5. She didn't know ________________ package to open first.

Write your own sentences.

1. ____
2. ____
3. ____

Answers: 1. Which 2. witch 3. witch 4. Which 5. which

wood / would

Study these words to learn their differences.

1 **wood** - the hard substance from trees and shrubs

a. The hall* leads to* a back porch made* of **wood**.
b. I don't know* whether* I should make my house out of **wood** or brick.
c. He threw* the piece* of **wood** into the fireplace.

2 **would** - used to show a wish, desire, or intent

a. How **would** you like your steak*—rare, medium, or well done?
b. "Which* **would** you like—coffee or tea?" asked the hostess.
c. **Would** you like me to* show you the way?

***Previously Used Words**

hall
to
made
know
whether
threw
piece
steak
which

PRACTICE EXERCISES

Write the correct word in the blank space. (Answers at bottom.)

1. ________________ you like to sit next to the window?
2. The ________________ crackled slowly in the fireplace.
3. I don't think that ________________ be a good idea.
4. What kind of salad dressing ________________ you like?
5. Let's go chop some ________________.

Write your own sentences.

1. ____
2. ____

Answers: 1. Would 2. wood 3. would 4. would 5. wood

SECTION THREE WORD REVIEW

Part A

DIRECTIONS: *Here are some of the new words covered in Section Three. Circle the one that fits best.*

1. Her father couldn't decide (which, witch) suit to buy.
2. The king's (rain, reign, rein) lasted only three years.
3. The professor forgot to call (role, roll).
4. Joe's (waist, waste) was 36 inches.
5. He drove a (stake, steak) into the ground.
6. The runner broke his (toe, tow) when he was tackled.
7. A trumpet doesn't have a (read, reed).
8. I have (to, too, two) much homework tonight.
9. The man made a (vain, vane, vein) attempt to save her life.
10. Bill (threw, through) the ball over the fence.
11. Our bridal (suite, sweet) was not what we had expected.
12. The child (read, red) the story to his aunt.
13. All he could do was (stair, stare) at his failing grade.
14. Are you sure (their, there, they're) not going to go?
15. It is important to (right, rite, write) English correctly.
16. The dog's (tail, tale) got caught in the door.
17. My (son, sun) went to Europe for the summer.
18. We went to a bargain (sail, sale).
19. She is a (vary, very) good boss to work for.
20. You should not (steal, steel) from other people.

SECTION THREE WORD REVIEW

Part B

DIRECTIONS: *Match the words with their definitions. Write the letter in front of the word.*

____ 1. weather	a. a sweet pastry
____ 2. sole	b. the truth; correct
____ 3. right	c. to inform in advance of danger or trouble
____ 4. road	d. the domination or power of a ruler
____ 5. war	e. trash
____ 6. sew	f. showing an economic loss
____ 7. right	g. the underneath part of a foot or shoe
____ 8. weak	h. true; correct
____ 9. seem	i. route; highway; street
____ 10. wood	j. struggle between opposing forces
____ 11. red	k. to put together by stitching
____ 12. roll	l. to guide or captain a ship
____ 13. scene	m. a large body of salt water; ocean
____ 14. waste	n. a place, position, or direction
____ 15. row	o. to give an impression
____ 16. warn	p. the hard substance from trees or shrubs
____ 17. reign	q. a single part of a play or movie
____ 18. where	r. not strong
____ 19. sea	s. to move a boat with oars
____ 20. sail	t. condition of the atmosphere

SECTION THREE WORD REVIEW

Part C

DIRECTIONS: Circle Right or Wrong for the proper usage of each bold word in the following sentences.

1. Have you **scene** her recently? Right / Wrong
2. The shoe had a very thin **sole**. Right / Wrong
3. The dog tried to **warn** its master. Right / Wrong
4. I'd like my **stake** rare, please. Right / Wrong
5. Are you going to the furniture **sale** today? Right / Wrong
6. The new student didn't **seem** to understand. Right / Wrong
7. The stock market prices began to **soar**. Right / Wrong
8. After his cold he looked very **weak**. Right / Wrong
9. In California it doesn't **rein** very much. Right / Wrong
10. Try not to **stare** at him. Right / Wrong
11. Fish were jumping in the **sea**. Right / Wrong
12. I hope the **whether** will be good tomorrow. Right / Wrong
13. Her **son** decided to go to college. Right / Wrong
14. Terry wanted the lead **role** in the play. Right / Wrong
15. The game was **vary** exciting. Right / Wrong
16. That actor is **vain**. Right / Wrong
17. Their cabin has a **wood** burning stove. Right / Wrong
18. I like to **reed** mystery novels. Right / Wrong
19. **Their** not coming to the dance. Right / Wrong
20. There were many rocks in the **rode**. Right / Wrong

COMPREHENSIVE WORD REVIEW

Part A: Matching

DIRECTIONS: *Match the words with their definitions. Write the letter in front of the word.*

____ 1. altar	a. grows in a garden
____ 2. warn	b. not a woman
____ 3. brake	c. head of a school
____ 4. capital	d. with nothing extra
____ 5. mail	e. to change
____ 6. alter	f. to look at for a long time
____ 7. flour	g. send a letter
____ 8. plain	h. you walk up or down it
____ 9. worn	i. a tool used for shaving or smoothing
____ 10. base	j. law or doctrine
____ 11. male	k. city, state or national power center
____ 12. flower	l. a short rest
____ 13. principal	m. low sound
____ 14. stair	n. used in many religions
____ 15. bass	o. to tell of danger
____ 16. plane	p. main government building
____ 17. break	q. to have put on clothes
____ 18. capitol	r. at the bottom
____ 19. stare	s. used to stop something
____ 20. principle	t. use it when baking

COMPREHENSIVE WORD REVIEW

Part B: Opposites

DIRECTIONS: *Match the word that means the opposite or nearly opposite. Write the letter in front of the word.*

____	1. night	a. strong
____	2. pair	b. read
____	3. right	c. subtract
____	4. son	d. uncle
____	5. flee	e. dressed
____	6. hair	f. sell
____	7. here	g. death
____	8. high	h. friendly
____	9. in	i. out; outside
____	10. add	j. not to run
____	11. fair	k. dig up; uncover
____	12. birth	l. dishonest
____	13. hostile	m. bald
____	14. aunt	n. low
____	15. bare	o. daughter
____	16. war	p. single
____	17. bury	q. day
____	18. weak	r. wrong
____	19. buy	s. there
____	20. write	t. peace

COMPREHENSIVE WORD REVIEW

Part C: Correct Word

Directions: Pick the correct word in parentheses and circle it.

1. The (air, err, heir) in big cities is usually polluted.
2. Her child started to (ball, bawl).
3. Two (dear, deer) ran (through, threw) the (due, do, dew) covered bushes.
4. It was a major historical (feat, feet).
5. Her voice was so (hoarse, horse) she couldn't sing.
6. I need to take out a (loan, lone) to purchase some (steel, steal).
7. The speaker's opinion tended to (vary, very) from the audience's.
8. Please don't (waste, waist) your money on that expensive (suite, sweet).
9. (Their, There, They're) not having much fun.
10. I like my (stake, steak) well done.
11. Professor Jackson never calls (role, roll).
12. She doesn't (seem, seam) to want another (peace, piece) of cake.
13. They are having a (sale, sail) at the market today.
14. The police went to the (cite, sight, site) of the murder.
15. I decided to (bi, buy, by, bye) a (gnu, new, knew) trash (bin, been).
16. It was a long (hall, haul) from Los Angeles to New York.
17. The entire village was in (morning, mourning).
18. (Wear, Where) are you going to (meat, meet) them?
19. (Hour, Our) house is (maid, made) of (wood, would).
20. I bruised my (right, write) (heal, heel) on the dirt (road, rode).

COMPREHENSIVE WORD REVIEW

Part D: Synonyms

DIRECTIONS: *Circle the letter that means the same or almost the same as the word on top.*

1. whole
   a. total of all the parts
   b. dig down in the ground
   c. a long walkway

2. week
   a. not strong
   b. seven days in a row
   c. 12 in a year

3. toe
   a. five on each hand
   b. five on each foot
   c. to pull something

4. tale
   a. something a dog wags
   b. a story
   c. position in a race

5. serial
   a. in a series
   b. breakfast food
   c. made from flour

6. hangar
   a. something you put clothes on
   b. an executioner
   c. a place to park airplanes

7. coarse
   a. not smooth; rough
   b. a path or trail to follow
   c. a class in school

8. boar
   a. not interesting
   b. to drill a hole in the ground
   c. a wild pig

9. dessert
   a. a dry, sandy area of land
   b. leave and not come back
   c. eat after dinner

10. merry
    a. what you do at a wedding
    b. happy; cheerful
    c. husband and wife

COMPREHENSIVE WORD REVIEW

Part D: Synonyms

11. heir
    a. something you breathe
    b. a mistake
    c. one who inherits something

12. fare
    a. conforming to rules
    b. impartial; honest
    c. a price charged for travel

13. grown
    a. to become mature; adult
    b. to show pain or grief
    c. adolescent

14. idyll
    a. worthless; without basis
    b. a symbol of worship
    c. peaceful prose or poetry

15. made
    a. a female servant
    b. to have done something
    c. to have started something

16. rowed
    a. to have moved a boat with oars
    b. past tense of ride
    c. route; highway; street

17. there
    a. relating to them
    b. a certain place or location
    c. they are

18. wood
    a. hard substance of trees
    b. used to show a wish
    c. a desire or intent

19. which
    a. sorceress
    b. one of a group
    c. a despiteful woman

20. weather
    a. an alternative
    b. having many choices
    c. condition of the atmosphere

COMPREHENSIVE WORD REVIEW

Part D: Synonyms

21. suite
    a. not bitter
    b. salty; sour
    c. connected rooms in a hotel

22. loan
    a. given for temporary use
    b. to give away
    c. alone; the only one

23. mete
    a. to get together
    b. flesh to be eaten
    c. to give out by measure

24. pain
    a. hurt
    b. a sheet of glass
    c. past tense of pay

25. principle
    a. person in authority
    b. law; doctrine
    c. director of a school

26. rote
    a. past tense of write
    b. to memorize without thinking
    c. to have spelled and composed

27. sow
    a. spread ideas
    b. to put together by stitching
    c. therefore

28. bare
    a. to carry something
    b. a heavy mammal
    c. naked; nude

29. beet
    a. red garden plant
    b. to win
    c. very tired; exhausted

30. break
    a. something to stop movement
    b. a short rest
    c. to cook something in the oven

COMPREHENSIVE WORD REVIEW

Part D: Synonyms

31. censor

    a. one who examines books

    b. an electric device

    c. one who collects pennies

32. dew

    a. to perform

    b. something owed as a debt

    c. condensed moisture

33. ferry

    a. male homosexual

    b. mythical person

    c. carry people or goods

34. flea

    a. very small insect

    b. to run from danger

    c. past tense of fly

35. hostile

    a. place to stay overnight

    b. easy to get along with

    c. unfriendly

36. male

    a. to send letters and postcards

    b. a boy or man

    c. the postal system

37. pale

    a. lacking color; pallid

    b. a bucket

    c. future tense of pull

38. piece

    a. part of the whole

    b. opposite of war

    c. friendly

39. role

    a. list of names

    b. part to be played

    c. to turn over and over

40. steak

    a. a marker in the ground

    b. something gained or lost

    c. a slice of meat or fish

ANSWERS

SECTION ONE WORD REVIEW

Part A *Page 41*	Part B *Page 42*	Part C *Page 43*
1. due	1. i	1. Wrong
2. beat	2. h	2. Wrong
3. deer	3. m	3. Wrong
4. bin	4. p	4. Right
5. damn	5. k	5. Wrong
6. bury	6. a	6. Wrong
7. coarse	7. l	7. Right
8. site	8. c	8. Right
9. cereal	9. n	9. Right
10. berth	10. r	10. Wrong
11. aunt	11. f	11. Right
12. scent	12. q	12. Right
13. censor	13. b	13. Right
14. err	14. e	14. Wrong
15. sell	15. j	15. Right
16. capital	16. d	16. Wrong
17. ad	17. s	17. Right
18. bear	18. g	18. Right
19. bass	19. t	19. Right
20. alter	20. o	20. Right

SECTION TWO WORD REVIEW

Part A *Page 95*	Part B *Page 96*	Part C *Page 97*
1. principal	1. l	1. Wrong
2. peak	2. h	2. Right
3. for	3. o	3. Right
4. won	4. g	4. Right
5. pray	5. j	5. Right
6. hall	6. b	6. Wrong
7. pane	7. k	7. Wrong
8. hoarse	8. c	8. Wrong
9. merry	9. n	9. Wrong
10. hostile	10. a	10. Wrong
11. maid	11. t	11. Wrong
12. whole	12. q	12. Right
13. meet	13. r	13. Right
14. pale	14. m	14. Wrong
15. flu	15. f	15. Wrong
16. hear	16. i	16. Right
17. plane	17. e	17. Wrong
18. knew	18. p	18. Right
19. flour	19. d	19. Wrong
20. groan	20. s	20. Wrong

SECTION THREE WORD REVIEW

Part A *Page 136*	Part B *Page 137*	Part C *Page 138*
1. which	1. t	1. Wrong
2. reign	2. g	2. Right
3. roll	3. h	3. Right
4. waist	4. i	4. Wrong
5. stake	5. j	5. Right
6. toe	6. k	6. Right
7. reed	7. b	7. Right
8. too	8. r	8. Right
9. vain	9. o	9. Wrong
10. threw	10. p	10. Right
11. suite	11. f	11. Right
12. read	12. a	12. Wrong
13. stare	13. q	13. Right
14. they're	14. e	14. Right
15. write	15. s	15. Wrong
16. tail	16. c	16. Right
17. son	17. d	17. Right
18. sale	18. n	18. Wrong
19. very	19. m	19. Wrong
20. steal	20. l	20. Wrong

COMPREHENSIVE WORD REVIEW

PART A: Matching

Page 139

1. n
2. o
3. s
4. k
5. g
6. e
7. t
8. d
9. q
10. r
11. b
12. a
13. c
14. h
15. m
16. i
17. l
18. p
19. f
20. j

PART B: Opposites

Page 140

1. q
2. p
3. r
4. o
5. j
6. m
7. s
8. n
9. i
10. c
11. l
12. g
13. h
14. d
15. e
16. t
17. k
18. a
19. f
20. b

COMPREHENSIVE WORD REVIEW

PART C: Correct Word

Page 141

1. air
2. bawl
3. deer, through, dew
4. feat
5. hoarse
6. loan, steel
7. vary
8. waste, suite
9. They're
10. steak
11. roll
12. seem, piece
13. sale
14. site
15. buy, new, bin
16. haul
17. mourning
18. Where, meet
19. Our, made, wood
20. right, heel, road

PART D: Synonyms

Page 142

1. a
2. b
3. b
4. b
5. a
6. c
7. a
8. c
9. c
10. b
11. c
12. c
13. a
14. c
15. b
16. a
17. b
18. a
19. b
20. c
21. c
22. a
23. c
24. a
25. b
26. b
27. a
28. c
29. a
30. b
31. a
32. c
33. c
34. a
35. c
36. b
37. a
38. a
39. b
40. c

INDEX

The words are listed in alphabetical order. The number after the word indicates the page on which the word, with definition, first appears.

INDEX